BILL RODGERS'

LIFETIME RUNNING PLAN

BILL RODGERS'

LIFETIME RUNNING PLAN

DEFINITIVE PROGRAMS FOR RUNNERS OF ALL AGES AND LEVELS

BILL RODGERS

with Scott Douglas

HarperPerennial

A Division of HarperCollins*Publishers*

This book includes treatments the author has found effective for some common running injuries. These treatments are not, however, intended to replace the services of a physician. All matters regarding your health require medical supervision.

A hardcover edition of this book was published in 1996 by HarperCollins Publishers.

HarperCollins books may be purchased for educational, business, or sales promotional use. For information please write to: Special Markets Department, HarperCollins Publishers, Inc., 10 East 53rd Street, New York, NY 10022.

First HarperPerennial edition published 1998.

Designed by Alma Hochhauser Orenstein

The Library of Congress has catalogued the hardcover edition as follows:

Rodgers, Bill, 1947–
Bill Rodgers' lifetime running plan / Bill Rodgers with Scott Douglas. — 1st ed.
p. cm.
ISBN 0–06–273386–9
1. Running. 2. Running—Training. I. Douglas, Scott. II. Title.
GV1061.R566 1996
796.42—dc20 96–13793

ISBN 0-06-273499-7 (pbk.)

98 99 00 01 02 ❖/RRD 10 9 8 7 6 5 4 3 2 1

To my wife, GAIL,
who is far stronger and more talented than I
in so many ways,
and who knows what counts most in life.

CONTENTS

ACKNOWLEDGMENTS

For the successful completion of this book, I must thank my coauthor, Scott Douglas, who kept me on a regular schedule of meetings for months, despite his commitment to his duties as senior writer at *Running Times* and his ambitious running program. In this endeavor, Scott showed world-class effort and persistence.

Also, thanks to our illustrator, Bob Carroll, and to Donn Kirk and Ben Grundstein, who provided the statistical charts in the appendix.

My special thanks for supporting our efforts to: Jeff Galloway, my Wesleyan University teammate and long-time friend; Dr. Walter Bortz, whose vision of the fit life and how to achieve it inspires me; Frank Shorter, my Olympic teammate and, in my opinion, the finest distance runner in American history, for writing the foreword and for more than 20 years of friendship; Grete Waitz and Joan Benoit Samuelson, long-time friends and fellow road warriors, and Don Kardong, one of our sport's most respected leaders, for their support; fellow runner Steve Stovall, of Mountain Lion Inc., for his gentle yet firm manner of leading me step by step to define this book; Robert Wilson, of HarperCollins, for believing in this project; and Elaine Verriest for guiding the project through production.

Without the love and support of my parents, Mr. and Mrs. Charles A. Rodgers Jr., I would never have been in the position to write this book. That also holds true for my brother, Charlie, and my sisters, Martha and Linda.

Finally, I'm a lucky man, not because I've won some races, have my health, or was able to write this book, but because Gail and I are the parents of Elise and Erika, who bring more happiness into our lives than anything else.

FOREWORD BY FRANK SHORTER

Bill Rodgers is an American running phenomenon. He has been continuously training and racing at a very high level of intensity for longer than anyone in the history of our sport. Because no runner has defied the gremlins of injury and burnout better than Bill has, I was eager to read this book.

Of course, I'm a little envious of Bill's staying power, but I realized long ago that he and I have developed separate but equal training routines. There's no danger to Bill of my totally adopting his methods; instead, I wanted to read out of respect and admiration. I was curious to see what aspects of his personality and approach would shine through, because I have always known that there's something about the way he incorporates running into his lifestyle that defines his unique ability to go on and on.

Bill points out the core knowledge of running theory is very basic. His presentations of the physiological, psychological and dietary aspects of training are very clear and well-grounded. I completely agree with his premise that the key to personal success is to adapt your training to your body and personality. This is good, sound information for beginner and expert alike.

As I continued to read, however, I realized that it's the tone and manner of Bill's presentation that are most significant. Bill has his own way of presenting himself and his ideas. I know this from all the running clinics we've done together over the years. But I had never really listened to him at length. After all, I was talking half the time during these clinics.

In this longer, written form, his thoughts emerge. It's how he both thinks about and reacts to what he's doing *as he does it* that makes him unique. Bill is almost a paradox: consistent but flexible in his approach to training, obsessive yet easy-going in his mental approach to his overall routine. I learned something from this book and have altered my own daily approach to running. I urge you to do the same.

Bill has written a book that contains sound information that will help runners of all levels improve their training and racing. He has also presented this information in a manner that is uniquely his. If you can pick up on some of the instinctive feel that Bill has for his craft and apply it to your training, you'll come a lot closer to maximizing your potential. None of us can duplicate what Bill has done, but he has opened up and presented himself in this book in a way that will allow all of us to run better.

INTRODUCTION

I'm writing this book because I read newspapers. This might sound odd, but stick with me. I was fortunate enough to have won the Boston and New York City Marathons four times each between 1975 and 1980, when the running boom was really taking off in this country. Ever since then, even though I've slowed with age, running has been at the core of my personal and professional lives. I attend more than 25 road races a year, I'm involved with running-related fundraisers for charities, I own a running store—a lot of my exposure to the world is through the filter of the running world. Based on that view, it appears the running boom is growing all the time, and that the fitness movement it spawned has reached every house in the U.S.

But like I said, I read newspapers. On the day I wrote this introduction, one of my local papers reported on a study published in the *Journal of the American Medical Association*. It brought me back to reality about the health of our country. Despite more than 20 years of reports on the massive and irrefutable evidence that regular exercise is the key to good physical and mental health, most Americans don't take care of themselves—22 percent get no exercise, and 54 percent exercise less than three times a week. Worse yet, the older the

Perrier
1

respondent in the study, the less likely that he or she got any exercise.

Now some of those people aren't going to exercise no matter what. However, many of them would like to, but have been misinformed. They think exercise is painful, complicated, time-consuming and expensive. They don't know that in just a few hours a week, they can revolutionize their lives with running. Yes, they probably know the physical benefits—the potentially dramatic weight loss and the protection from coronary artery disease and some forms of cancer, for example. They might even believe running would give them more energy. But most of what they've heard about exercise hasn't mentioned the intangible benefits, such as feelings of accomplishment, relaxation and self confidence, that can have at least as profound an effect on people's lives as the many physical benefits. They don't know that running is freedom.

So I've written this book in the hopes of reaching these people. I want to show not only that running *can* be enjoyable, but that it *should* be enjoyable. And I want to show that with one thought that underlies everything in the book: if you explore what running has to offer, if you really give it a chance, you'll discover some facet of the sport that speaks to you. When you find that, you've found the key, because you'll want to keep pursuing it, and you'll want to run for the rest of your life.

Running for a lifetime can take many forms. You'll probably develop your own permutations of many of them throughout your running life. In all of them, though, you're going to have one shared goal—keep going. How that's done is different, depending on what your emphasis is. That's why this book is structured as it is. No matter where you are in your running life, there's a chapter that you can jump right into and find your needs addressed. This book is meant to be more of a lifelong resource than an all-in-one-sitting read. You can come back to it again and again and find how to apply my basic principles of the sport to whatever your current approach is. Within some of the chapters, I've included short profiles of some runners who embody some of the themes of that chapter. Read about them, and I think you'll see some of yourself in your present situation.

Still, after more than 30 years at it, I know running can't be compartmentalized that easily. After reading the chapter that first appeals to you, visit the others. You'll learn how to keep your running simple, fun and successful. Once you do that, nothing can stop you.

This book includes treatments that the author has found effective for some common running injuries. These treatments are not, however, intended to replace the services of a physician. All matters regarding your health require medical supervision.

Getting Started

THE BASICS OF BEGINNING

The advice I have for beginners is of the same philosophy that I have for runners of all levels of experience and ability—consistency, a sane approach, moderation and making your running an enjoyable, rather than dreaded part of your life.

NOT FOR BEGINNERS ONLY

Don't let the title of this chapter fool you. Although my primary emphasis in it is to guide beginners toward a lifetime of running, there's plenty here that nonnovices can learn from. To some degree, your running career starts anew every day. It's easy to get cocky about your running, and to think that you know all that there is to know. It's also easy to get in certain routines or habits that aren't the best for your long-term enjoyment of running, and to stay in them mostly because you've forgotten some of the fundamentals. For me, at least, even after 30 years in the sport, I still make mistakes and occasionally think that some of the basic rules don't apply to me. While writing this chapter, I was surprised by how much of what I have to say to beginners applies to all runners, myself included.

The advice I have for beginners is of the same philosophy that I have for runners of all levels of experience and ability—consistency, a sane approach, moderation, making your running an enjoyable rather than dreaded part of your life, etc. Yes, there's material in this chapter that long-time runners will find to be rudimentary, but there are also many basic truths about running that everyone can benefit being reminded of. So even if you're not a beginner, I suggest you at least skim this chapter to get a better understanding of my basic approach to a lifetime of running. Then, when reading later chapters, you'll better appreciate how to make use of what I'm telling you.

HOW TO GET STARTED

Before I can tell you how to start running, you should be able to say why you want to start running. That's because to get going systematically, you need goals. Do you want to lose weight? To regain the energy you used to have? To feel better about yourself? To get ready for a race? There are infinite reasons to start running, but you'll increase your chances of sticking with it if, at the outset, you can determine what your short-term and long-term goals are.

Your short-term goals should be fairly precise—you want to be able to mark real progress toward them. Short-term can mean as short as within a week, but don't let your goals take longer than 3 months to reach. Otherwise, you might lose interest in the early going, which can be the toughest time of a lifetime of running. You want your short-term goals to give you the motivation to keep running so that your long-term goals can become realities.

Everyone is going to have different goals. Let's say you're a smoker, like I was when I started running again in the early 1970s. My short-term goals were very short. I would tell myself, "Today, I'm only going to smoke five cigarettes." The more I would run, the more I would gradually reduce the number of cigarettes I would smoke. After a run, I wouldn't want to smoke for a long time, so I would construct my day such that because of this positive force in my life (my running), the negative force (my smoking) would be harder to do or be less appealing.

Another way to help yourself stick with this new, positive force in your life is to put yourself in an environment where you'll find like-minded people. When I started running again, I joined the local YMCA. It had an indoor track, light weights, a swimming pool, rowing machines—it was good for me to see other people who had made a commitment to the same thing that I was trying to do. I met a couple runners

HOW MUCH AT FIRST?

As with so many things in running, there's no universal standard for how much you should run at the beginning of your program. We tend to think in miles, so if you're doing your running on a track or another calibrated site, it's natural to have an initial goal of, say, half a mile, a mile, 2 miles, etc. But you don't have to worry about precisely measuring your distance—your goal could also be to run around the block, to run for 15 minutes, etc.

Whether you're measuring by time or distance, I'd advise two important rules for runners in the first month of their programs. First, don't mix the two when you're starting out. That is, if you're starting with one mile at a time, don't clock yourself. Just concentrate on covering the distance consistently at a comfortable level of effort. In the same way, if you're running based on time, don't keep pushing yourself to cover more ground in that time. When you're a new runner, you want to do what experienced runners call "laying a base"—putting in time on your feet, building your endurance, but doing so comfortably, without regard for how hard you're working. If you want, there can be plenty of time for that later; for now, though, lay your base.

Second, don't go beyond 30 minutes or 3 miles at a time during your first month of running. Yes, you may be able to do more, perhaps even from day one, but remember: your number one goal is to develop consistency. The only way to do that is to develop a moderate training program. If you overdo it at first, you're more likely to get injured or burnt out. Beginning runners can be more susceptible to injuries than long-timers, because new runners' muscles, tendons, ligaments and bones aren't as used to working hard. You might also be carrying extra weight, and this will add to the stress that's put on your body.

When I started running in high school, I would run for 10 to 20 minutes. Even by my senior year, when I was the state champion in cross country, most of my runs were 3 miles long. When I graduated, the longest run I had ever done was 12 miles, and I thought that was a megadistance run. This sensible, gradual progression is what allowed me to run well later—I was continually improving, I wasn't getting hurt, and I wasn't getting frustrated or tired of it.

In contrast, a friend of mine, Patti Lyons Catalano (now Dillon), once held the American record in the marathon, but she started out like most people—on her own without good advice. She thought that running should hurt, and that the more she hurt, the more this meant that she was doing it right. So on her first run, she ran 7 miles! After that, she was so sore she couldn't run for a week. When she was able to again, she ran 7 miles again, and suffered the same fate after. Eventually, her body adjusted, and she didn't have to wait a week between runs, but think how much more quickly she would have progressed, and how much more she would have enjoyed her running, if she had held back.

Also, don't think, like Patti did, that it's running or nothing. If you need to mix running and walking, that's fine. If you need to start with walking only, that's fine. It doesn't matter what pace you're going as long as it feels like an effort for you. Everything you do as a beginner is a lift up from nothing. As you become stronger, you'll sense when you can add more running without having to work harder than you used to have to walk. Those days—when you begin to see the rewards of your work—can be some of the most satisfying in a lifetime of running.

there who talked about the Boston Marathon. I had no idea that I would eventually win Boston; it was just great support to be around kindred spirits.

Easing into It

You'll likely also have a short-term goal that relates to the time or distance that you can run, such as running 20 minutes nonstop. It might take you a few weeks to get there, or you might be able to do that right away. Everyone is different. Don't have a preconceived notion of how quickly you should progress. If you rush it, you'll increase your chances of getting hurt, and if you allow yourself to get frustrated by how you're progressing, you're more likely to give up. You have the rest of your life to keep increasing your fitness.

The key is to be consistent. By that I mean getting out to run about four times a week. That's a good sign that, more often than not, you're consciously deciding to improve your life.

At all times in your running life, but especially when you're beginning, it's more important not to overdo it than to underdo it. You want to ease into your running, both on a daily basis and in an overall sense. Because of bad memories from gym class and inaccurate portrayals of running by the mass media, a lot of people assume that running is supposed to hurt. So when they're out of breath while they're running and very sore afterward, they figure that they must be doing it right. They don't know that most long-time runners find their running to be pleasant, that they carry on lengthy conversations while they run, and that they usually feel better after running than during any other part of the day.

Gauging Effort

If you can, find a friend of a similar level of fitness as yours to start running with. You're more likely to stick with your plan for a given day if you've made a commitment to someone to meet him or her at a certain place at a certain time. This is especially the case if, like many beginning runners, the best time for you to run is in the morning before work. Knowing that someone will be waiting for me is sometimes the only thing that gets me out of bed.

Another good reason to have someone to run with is that

doing so makes it easy to determine if you're working too hard. Like I said, at first you want all of your running to be at a moderate level of effort. If you're running with someone, you can gauge this by taking the famous "talk test": if you can't carry on a conversation while you're running, then you're going too fast. (On the other hand, if you can peel off minutes-long soliloquies, you might want to pick up the pace a bit.)

If you're like most beginners, however, you'll be starting out on your own. Then, gauging your effort can be trickier. (You're probably already worried that your neighbors will think you're crazy, so you don't want to add to their suspicions by taking the talk test when you're by yourself.) First, even though I've stressed that running isn't supposed to be nonstop agony, accept that there will be a certain amount of discomfort. That just comes with moving from being unfit to being fit. At the right level of effort, this discomfort will be a slight shortness of breath, and your muscles will feel a little heavy, especially at the beginning of a run.

There are specific discomforts that are warning signs—a sharp pain in one leg, a side ache, feeling as out of breath as if you're sprinting for a bus. These are all messages from your body that you're overdoing it. If you ease into each day's run, your heart rate will elevate gradually, and after about 5 minutes, you should be able to pick up the pace a bit, if you want. Many beginning runners can't believe they should feel better 10 minutes into their run than they did at the start. If you don't, that means you're starting too fast. Give yourself some time to get going, allow what I call the "perspiration effect" to occur—your body has warmed up and is moving more comfortably, and you're on your way to discovering how enjoyable running can be.

Progressing Systematically

Be neither limited nor intimidated by your long-term goals—as you make progress toward your short-term goals, it's likely that you'll revise your long-term ones. You'll discover what parts of running you like the most, what your capabilities are, how often you like to run, how it best works into your schedule, etc. You may have started out with a long-term goal of being able to run a 5-mile charity race in 3 months, and find that you're able to cover the distance after just 2 months of running. Great. There's nothing that says you must stick to your original plan. Run the race you originally scheduled to gain a deserved sense of accomplishment, but in the meantime, devise a new goal, such as building up to being able to run for more than an hour nonstop, so you can keep that feeling of progression.

Or maybe you wanted to lose 15 pounds after 3 months of running, but have lost 10. Emphasize the positive. You've started to revolutionize your life—don't let 5 pounds come between you and continuing to do so. Perhaps you haven't been running as much as you had hoped to, or you need to watch your diet more, or your original goal was unrealistic. (Some beginners find they don't lose weight as rapidly as they'd like when they start running. In some instances, especially with light-framed women, they're gaining some muscle as they become more fit. Don't assume that all weight loss is good, or that all weight gain is bad. It's fat, not just nondescript weight, that you want to lose.) Whatever the reason, revise your goal. Recognize your accomplishment of beginning to get fit and losing a good chunk of weight, and plan how to get to the next level.

Once you've reached a basic level of running fitness—you can run nonstop 20 to 30 minutes, four times a week—you can start thinking about adding variety to your training. Note that I didn't say that you *have* to. The greatest gains in health and fitness come from moving from being sedentary to this minimum level of activity. If you're content with this amount of running, don't let anybody make you feel inadequate about it. You're doing more than most people are to take care of yourself. You're a runner.

But most people will find that they'll want to explore a little, whether in terms of pace, distance, terrain, or some combination. As in the rest of life, variety is the spice of training. As I'll discuss soon, I admit that running can be boring, especially if you let it become so. So continually find new ways to challenge yourself. Racing is an obvious solution. Even after racing as long as I have, I still find it captivating: the test of how good I can be on that day, the struggle to improve month by month as the season progresses, the camaraderie of runners of all levels of ability running the same course at the same time. To me, it's the greatest party in the world.

But let's assume that, for now, you don't want to race. There are still a number of ways to vary your training. Once a week, tack on extra distance to your usual run. Start by adding one third of your regular mileage, and keep adding thirds until you've doubled your normal run. For example, if you usually run 3 miles, run 4 one day a week. The next week, try 5 miles, and once you can do that, go for 6. These longer runs will not only give you new, quantifiable goals, but the endurance that you'll gain trying to do them will make your regular runs feel easier.

Of course, you can increase the length of your regular runs as well. The common rule is not to increase your weekly mileage by more than 10 percent. That is, if you're running 20 miles a week, don't do more than 22 miles the next week. As we know, though, rules are made to be broken. Some beginners, especially young runners, might be able to increase by 20 percent a week. Everyone is a little different. I base all my running decisions on how I feel—can I handle upping my mileage by 10 percent? How much more fatigued will I feel? Should I stay at this level for 2 more weeks, then increase? These are the kinds of questions you should ask yourself. As I keep saying, the best long-term approach is a moderate one. Don't increase your mileage week after week after week. Beyond a certain point, you'll get injured, and you'll start to regret, rather than enjoy, your running.

I'll grant that after all of my running, I have a better innate sense of how increasing my mileage will affect how I feel than most beginners do. But I had to experiment just like everybody else, and I still do, especially as I make adjustments for age. That's one of my favorite things about running—you're always learning about yourself and what your capabilities are. I didn't do my first 15-mile run until I was in college. I had already been running for years, but it still knocked me back a bit. You want to have something left in the tank at the finish, both on a given day and at the end of the week. As a beginning runner trying to add distance, it's okay to end your runs a little more tired than usual, but you shouldn't be fall-down tired, as if you've given a supreme effort. Save something for later—your goal is to progress sanely.

Other Forms of Variety

Another variable you can play with is speed. Once a week, push the pace on your regular run. See what it feels like to work a little harder than you have been. If you time yourself, you'll probably find that week to week your time for the route will decline. I know few better feelings in running. That's the essence of our sport—human performance.

And don't be afraid to run in different places. Many beginners get used to running just one or two routes. Most days, that's fine, because you should pick out the courses that are pleasant for you, and a familiar course can make a run seem to pass more quickly on the inevitable tougher days.

(More on that in a moment.) But one of the greatest things about running, which few other sports offer to this degree, is its freedom of alternative training sites. You can run almost anywhere—city streets, suburban neighborhoods, country roads, wooden trails, beaches, mountains, tracks, fields—the options are endless. People have run marathons in the Antarctic! Can you go play football in the middle of the woods? No, but I can call up a friend, and we can go crashing through the woods near my house, and have an interesting run. So when you want to run someplace different, do so. And don't feel guilty, especially on the days of your longer runs, to drive somewhere special, such as a state park, to run. If people drive there to eat and play on swings, surely you can justify driving there to run.

DEBUNKING EXCUSES FOR NOT RUNNING

In the 30 years I've been a runner I've run more than 150,000 miles. Still, some of the hardest steps I take are those first few getting out the door for daily runs.

So I know what it's like to have a hard time getting going, and I sympathize with people who feel that way about running in general, not just running on a given day. I continually meet people who say that they *want* to start running or some other form of exercise, *but*. . . Then they give one or more excuses, nearly all of which I've heard countless times. Here are some of the most common reasons I hear from people about why they don't exercise, and what I try to tell them in response.

Excuse #1: I Don't Have Time

Usually, someone who says that he or she doesn't have time for exercise has never made it a part of their life. They don't understand what it is to feel fit. There are many, many people with very busy lives—they're parents, they run businesses, they volunteer in their communities—but they know that the tiny amount of time they spend running gives them a return that is monumental.

The physical and psychological strength they derive from running increases the amount of "time" in their lives. That is, when you think of time, what do you do with your time? How much energy do you have in your time? How good do you feel in your 24 hours a day? If you think that you don't have the time, it's likely you don't realize the huge paybacks in quality of time that come through the small amount invested in working out.

"Okay," I often hear at this point, "you've convinced me that I should try it. But how do I squeeze it in?"

Look at your day and your current schedule and be honest about what you're doing with your time. Do you really have no time at all? You can't give up half an hour of watching television to feel better than you ever have? Are you really working all the time? If so, I certainly can't say otherwise, but think about the president. He's one of the busiest people in the world, with one of the world's most important jobs, yet he understands that getting out to run most days is important and helps him do his job better. In fact, three of our last four presidents have been runners. Perhaps realizing this will help you take a closer look at your situation.

Find the time in the day that's best for you. The morning is good for many working runners with busy lives. Running in the morning before work gives you abundant energy for the rest of the day, and you won't find yourself at the end of the day fatigued from a tough day at work and still having to get in a run. Indeed, several studies of working athletes have shown a higher rate of compliance among morning exercisers; it's easier to get diverted at the end of the day and to come up with excuses why your workout isn't as important.

Maybe you can find the time at work. When I was a teacher and training for the Olympic Marathon, I asked for and received permission to run during my lunch hour. Perhaps you can get extra time at lunch and leave work a little later. Or maybe you can run after work from your office, so that when you get home, you're done exercising for the day and can concentrate on your family and home responsibilities.

Whenever it is that you decide to set aside to run, it's important that you and those around you understand the central importance of this time, and how it will improve your quality of life. Don't let the clock overwhelm you—keep your running easy to do. I recently met a runner who was telling me how he had just started his own business and had a young child, and he couldn't seem to fit in his running. "I can't come home from work and tell my wife that I'm going out for a 10-mile run," he told me. "Fine," I said. "Go out for half an hour—you'll get most of the benefits." If you make it too hard, you're going to find it that much easier to stop.

Once you've taken a step, you're there. As an ex-smoker, I know this feeling well. You've made the decision that you're going to have control over this part of your life and that this is just for you; from that, you get a great sense of empowerment. After a short while, you realize it isn't as hard as you thought it would be, which is that much more motivating. You realize no matter how busy you are, carving out this time to run is not extra-life; it's normal life, and increases the quality of all the rest of your time.

Excuse #2: I'm Too Tired

I feel the same way.

Seriously, people are tired for different reasons—they have poor diets, they make bad lifestyle choices, they're overworked just to make ends meet, etc.—but many people are tired simply because they have no basic level of fitness. In other words, they have a "normal" level of fitness, which is to say, none.

Again, I used to smoke before I started running again in the early '70s, and I think deciding to quit cigarettes is analogous to deciding to give running a try. You say to yourself, "Here's this major thing in my life that I want to change. It's not for my boss, it's not for my wife or my husband or my grandfather or anybody else. This is something that I'm doing for myself." When you look at it that way, you're more likely to give it a try.

"But why would I want to spend any time exercising?" people ask me. "I'm tired already. I'll just become more tired if I run." That's not true. You become more energized as you become fitter; you feel better throughout the day. Research backs this up, as do the practices of businesses. Dean Witter, for example, asks potential employees what their sports habits are. They like people who are runners and, strange as it may seem, golfers. They recognize that both groups of athletes are people who do this substantial thing on their own, that they're people who took the initiative to undertake their sport with the understanding they'd get this great return from it.

Look at the reasons why you're tired. Ask yourself whether it's acceptable to have a "normal" level of fitness, when the normal pulse rate is 72 beats per minute. That's the pulse of a sick society. You have to come to the point where you say, "What's the future for me? Am I going to look and feel and live like this for the next 30 years? Am I going to accept this low quality of life? Or can I change? Can I become more fit at age 55 than I was 30 years ago?"

Fitness is a gift. It's better than a million dollars in the bank. If you can get that gift and explore it for yourself, then no one person or group can take that gift from you. Everyone has that potential. I love to see people change their lives and say, "I am an athlete. I can do this." That's the most powerful feeling in the world.

Excuse #3: It Will Ruin My Knees

In traveling all over the country, I meet people everywhere who don't know about the long-term effects of running. They seem almost convinced that I'm lying when I say that my knees don't bother me. The running and fitness boom notwithstanding, our sport has a terrible image in the U.S., thanks largely to the mass media, who don't understand running and encourage people to think of being "normal"—that is, out of shape and probably overweight—as desirable.

Not many organizations have made headway in overcoming running's negative image, despite the fact that research shows that, generally speaking, muscles, tendons, ligaments and bones get stronger with weight-bearing exercise. When I think about some of my encounters with medical doctors, it's easy to understand (but not to accept) why more people don't know this, because even some doctors seem ignorant of the long-term benefits of running. For example, a doctor approached me recently and asked me whether I was concerned about hypertrophy (enlargement) of the heart, and if I wasn't, why I wasn't, because I should be. In other words, here was a trained medical professional who thinks running is going to kill you. It's no wonder that in a society that worships doctors most people honestly believe they're doing their bodies more long-term good by staying sedentary than by using them.

I often meet ex-runners who have given up because they say they had an injury that they couldn't shake. Yes, injuries are part of our sport. Most of us have weak spots on our bodies that will be targeted when overdoing it. In talking with many of these people, I discover that they made many of the same mistakes: they tried to run too far, too fast, too soon, and often in the wrong shoes. The key is to learn how to train effectively, so that your running is challenging and enjoyable without you overdoing it. Read as much as you can about the sport, and talk with experienced runners. You'll likely find someone who has had the same injury, and if he or she can still run, why can't you? Learn not only how to treat injuries, but how to prevent them.

Excuse #4: I'm Not an Athlete. I Can't Run Around the Block.

You might not be able to run around the block, but you can walk around it. Then you could move to mixing walking and running, and gradually increasing the amount of time you spend running as you notice the dramatic improvements that just doing something—*anything*—causes in your fitness. There's always something you can do.

Don't let our society's standard notion of what an athlete is intimidate you. We are assaulted by continual images of the technique sports, the fast-twitch muscle fiber sports that rely on quick explosions of muscular power, such as football, basketball, baseball, etc. Recognize that by becoming an endurance athlete, that you are in the minority, but a very fit minority.

Think about it: you might be 65 years old and able to outrun just about anybody in the NBA. I was once on a television show in Charlotte, North Carolina, which is where Michael Jordan is from. The television interviewer said to me, "Well, Bill, I guess you didn't make as much money as Michael Jordan did this year." "Yeah," I said, "but I can whip him good in a road race." With just a little bit of regular training, so can you.

People who think they aren't athletes tell me they're embarrassed to be seen exercising in public. I understand that feeling. When I returned to running after quitting for 2½ years, I felt odd, because I had never really run through the city before. I felt stupid going out in running gear, so at first I did my training on an indoor track. Finally, I went to a park that was about a mile away, and there I could relax more. If you feel self-conscious, go to an environment where others are working out, such as a park, bike path or fitness center.

And when you do go to where other runners are, don't worry if it seems like you're surrounded by young, hard bodies. Half of all runners are over the age of 40, and more than 30 percent of runners are women. The diversity of running is what makes it unique—in most other sports, you don't see a great deal of people participating past the age of 25. In running, you'll see a variety of ages out there, from kids to people in their 70s and older. There's camaraderie in this, because you'll realize that despite our youth-oriented society, you can feel good about being a runner at whatever age you are, and possibly be fitter than you ever have been, not to mention fitter than many 25-year-olds!

Decide what you want to do with your running. Don't listen to people who say your running isn't legitimate unless you run a marathon. I don't believe that; I do believe in easing into things. If you want to run a race at some point, that's great—races are a wonderful way to break up your everyday running, and you can meet many kindred spirits who will help you realize you're not as weird as other people might have you believe. But you don't have to run races to be an athlete. If you're out there exercising your God-given capabilities, then you're an athlete. Tell them I said so.

Jill Kutcher: Everyone Is an Athlete

Americans are conditioned to believe that the only athletes over the age of 23 are the millionaires they see on television playing in one massive arena or another. That's a shame, because, as the ads say, life isn't a spectator sport. One of the great things about running is that, with just a little exposure to it, you're encouraged to develop and explore your physical capabilities. In other words, you realize that everyone can be an athlete.

Consider Jill Kutcher, of Reading, Massachusetts. A 26-year-old account executive for a direct marketing firm, Jill runs 3 miles, three to five times a week, and, for now at least, has sworn off racing. Based on this, most people would classify Jill as a "jogger," "fitness runner," or some other term nonrunners use to benignly belittle significant effort. (Since I retired from marathons, several journalists have labeled me a "fun runner," despite the 25 races I run each year!) But listen to what motivated Jill to start running.

"My boyfriend runs, and in the spring of 1994 I thought it would be fun to run with him," she says. "I had been doing aerobics for five years, so I thought that I wouldn't have any problem. I thought I was in good shape. But I couldn't keep up with him. I was surprised at how hard running just one mile turned out to be. I didn't like not being good at it, and I resolved that I would get to where I could say that I could run three miles whenever I wanted."

At 5'7", 120 pounds, Jill didn't care about losing weight when she started running. Instead, like any athlete, she had a performance goal, and wanted to challenge herself to meet it. She gradually built her mileage, and by the summer of 1995, she could comfortably handle 4 miles, five times a week. She cuts back some during the winter, when it's late and dark when she gets home from work, but, like all athletes, still tests herself. "Running is different from something like aerobics, which got really boring," she says. "You can always try to go farther or faster, you can try to run with someone who you haven't run with before, things like that."

Jill recognizes very real benefits from her modest program. "I like feeling healthy, and I always feel better after I run," she says. "If I've had a stressful day at work, there's no better way to clear my mind." Still, as with so many runners, Jill is first and foremost an athlete, regardless of how the rest of society defines that term. "You know what I like best about running?" she asks. "I like to talk with others and tell them what I can do physically."

WHAT TO EXPECT

One of running's many attributes is that you can do it as much on your own as you like. You don't have to join a league, or coordinate tee times with others, or wait for the pool to open. If you want, it can be just you and the roads.

As wonderful as this autonomy and flexibility is, though, it can also be a problem for many beginners. If you always run by yourself, or if you never talk to other runners, or read about running, it's likely some things will happen in your running that will take you by surprise, and not always pleasantly so. Many a beginner has quit after making a great deal of progress in a short time because they thought that something had gone wrong with their running or, worse, them.

Usually, however, these "surprises" are par for the course. Here are some common developments that strike runners throughout their careers, but especially after the exciting initial gains are made. I'm not implying that they aren't significant, or that you shouldn't pay attention to them, but don't let them scare you into thinking something drastic is wrong.

Expect a Certain Amount of Boredom

Not every run is going to be a revelatory experience on a warm spring day in the freshly-flowered woods. In our society, we're conditioned to think we should be entertained, even stimulated, all the time. Well, in reality, running, just like anything else, can be tedious. I don't make too much of this.

Isn't even the greatest job like that sometimes? What on this earth isn't?

People worry too much about this issue. I think about it like I think about marriage or raising children—it isn't continually exciting, there are going to be hard times, but you know it's something you really want to do and you're doing it toward a positive end.

A plus, compared to marriage or raising children, is that if you want to take a break from your routine, you can feel free to do so. Breaks can take different forms for different types of runners. For a beginner, it might mean not running for a week, and returning refreshed. For a long-time runner, it might mean cutting back his or her mileage, or racing at unusual distances. This is also a good time to experiment with other aerobic sports, such as cycling, in-line skating, or swimming. The fitness you've gained from running will have made you strong enough to try other activities without feeling as if you're starting over.

The way I find around my boredom is going to races. Races add a dimension to running that a regular runner who is always on his or her own can't experience. Almost everybody who goes to races would tell nonracers they're missing out, that this is what it's all about. Fitness and health are running's great bonuses, but racing adds an excitement that's hard to get elsewhere in your life. You can test your very limits; you can discover things about yourself that your regular life would never have revealed to you; you can be your own hero—it's hard to do that on a daily training run.

And you don't have to become a hardcore racer to get these benefits. One of the best ways to beat boredom is to run with others. If you usually run 3 miles a day, why not run at your normal pace, but in an organized 5K race? See what it's like and if this is a dimension of running that you want to include in your program. You're likely to meet other people of your level of fitness, and maybe meet some potential run-

ning partners. For older runners especially, whose busy lives might give them little time to make new acquaintances, the ease with which runners make friends with one another can go far to relieve some of the tedium.

Racing is also a big help because it will help you to develop a seasonal approach toward your running. For example, I run about 25 races a year. My last races for the year are usually in November, and by then I'm ready to back off and change the emphasis of my running. Throughout December and January, I pretty much do just steady mileage—going out and running moderately, like most beginners. By the time these 2 months are over, I'm eager to introduce more variety in my running, and I start racing and doing some harder training to prepare for the spring racing season. Come summer, I back off a bit in my mileage and run mostly shorter races, such as 5Ks, so the heat doesn't drain me too much. As the weather cools, I start doing more mileage and prepare for 10Ks and half marathons. After all that, I look forward to low-keying my approach, and I start the cycle again with my relaxed running in December. Sure, there are still days within each season in which I might be bored, but by having different emphases in my running throughout the year, I'm able to stay very interested in it most of the time.

Finally, one of the best motivators I know is injury. There's nothing like having something taken away from you to make you realize how much you love it. There are many great things in my life, but if I can't have that buttress there that running is for me, other things lose some of their luster. If you find that you're taking your running for granted, think what your life would be like without it.

Expect Plateaus

Your initial gains in fitness come quickly. After all, everything you do is an improvement over what you were doing when you were sedentary. But after awhile—it can be as short as in 2 or 3 months—you'll hit patches in which your improvements will become increasingly harder to recognize. At times, you might even feel as if you're going backwards.

Plateaus are easy to explain; don't let them get you down. Strange as it may seem, the fitter you are, the more common plateaus are. Remember, the greatest gains in health and fitness come when moving from doing nothing to doing anything. After that, the law of diminishing returns sets in. Tangible progress becomes increasingly harder to recognize, especially if you're not racing. Once you've attained that basic level of fitness that comes through half an hour of running four times a week, it's likely you'll notice progress in the form of breakthroughs. That is, seemingly out of the blue, you'll feel as comfortable running 8½-minute miles as you used to be running 9-minute miles. That's a sign you're on the right track—your body is adjusting to your gradual approach to building fitness. In 1974, I ran 2:19 at the Boston Marathon. The following year, after consistently, but moderately, increasing my training, I ran 2:09 and won the race. Your breakthrough will probably not be as dramatic, but it can be as exciting.

If, in contrast to the expected plateaus, you feel as if your fitness is declining, this means that your body isn't adjusting to your training. There are any number of reasons for this phenomenon, nearly all of which are discernible if you pay attention to the messages your body is sending you and evaluate everything in your life. Are you getting enough sleep? Are you eating properly? Has work or your personal life been unusually stressful? Have you been around children or coworkers who have been sick? Generally, in our society we ignore these subtle messages from our bodies, but now that you're an athlete, you need to pay them greater heed. When beginning runners notice backward progress, it means they're trying to do too much too soon given the other stresses in their lives. Back off to half your normal distance, or take a few days off, and you'll probably promptly return to your former level of fitness.

Expect Some Soreness

Earlier I said that running shouldn't hurt much. That doesn't mean it's always going to be pain free. You're likely to be more sore than you might like during your first stages of running. Again, it's important to distinguish between a small amount of overall soreness, especially in your legs, and acute pain in a specific body part that becomes more noticeable the more you run. Don't think of a little soreness after a run as a negative thing; it's a sign you're using muscles that aren't used to being exercised. If you stick with it using the moderate progression I've been preaching, they'll adapt. Give yourself 3 to 6 months in which to expect this low-level, post-run tenderness.

Also, don't be worried by the occasional blister or hot spot on a foot. As with your muscles, your feet are being asked to do more than they're used to. Blisters, at least, are easily treatable with moleskin, different socks or different shoes. As with any specific hurt that you notice on a run, the key is to take quick action. You can almost always run through the little aches, and as you run more, you'll learn more about which ones you can do that with. But if you can, cut your run short and tend to the hurt immediately. If it's a muscle ache, ice the area that hurts for 10 to 15 minutes as soon as possible after finishing, then ice it again before you go to sleep.

The more you watch yourself, the more you save yourself future aggravation. Just like it's the people who take charge of their health who usually see doctors the least, runners who are attentive to the little details of aches and pains usually get injured the least. When what started as a little soreness escalates into something that bothers you in your everyday activities, or gets worse as you run, you've let it go too far, and you need to cut back until the pain subsides.

Expect Hot Weather to Drain You

To me, the summer has always been the hardest time of the year. If you live in an area that has high temperatures or humidity—or worse, both simultaneously—expect some pretty unusual fatigue, and not just when you're running. When you exercise in the heat, of course, you'll know why you're probably struggling more to run your normal distance or pace. As your core body temperature rises, so does your sweat rate, and you become dehydrated. This lowers the amount of blood in your heart and decreases the volume of blood that your heart can deliver with each beat. As a result, your heart rate increases, and a given level of performance becomes more difficult to maintain.

But you'll probably also struggle more from day to day. Because of the chronic effects of dehydration, it's tougher to feel as if you're recovering from one run to the next. Your legs will be sorer and your overall energy level will be lower. Accept that the heat is going to take its toll on you, but also learn how to cope with it. Run during the cooler times of the day, back off in pace and distance, start your runs slower than in cool weather, and drink small amounts of fluid every waking hour. During the summer, check the color of your urine frequently to see that it's clear.

Expect Changes in How You Feel from Day to Day

You'll usually know why you're more tired than usual on a given day—you've been traveling a lot, you've had a tough time at work, you ran harder or farther than usual 2 days ago, etc. But you're also subject to a vaguer, more long-term rollercoaster effect in how you feel from day to day. Fifteen to 20 years ago, the big talk was about the "runner's high." Now we know that this "high," or feeling of joyous effortlessness that can accompany running, is caused by the release in our brains of chemicals called endorphins. We're learning that emotional matters can also have a chemical basis, and that mental stress, whether good or bad, can have a profound impact on your physical performance.

I know that if I've had an exciting day—such as finding out about an upcoming trip, or learning that one of my daughters has done well in school—I get a boost of energy, and no matter how tired I was feeling, I feel great on my run. In the same way, even if you've been feeling great in your training, but you receive some bad news, your run will probably be more of a struggle. Sometimes the things that affect you will be more subtle, and you might not be able to discern why you feel as you do. Accept the fact that you're going to feel different from day to day, even if you regularly run the same course at the same pace at the same time of day.

Tom Heeter: A Bit of Effort, a World of Difference

It's common to start running to get in shape. It's uncommon, however, for a dog to provide the motivation.

In September 1994, Tom Heeter, of Randallstown, Maryland, was walking the family dog, Cinnamon. On a whim, he decided to run a bit with Cinnamon. "A bit" turned out to be just one block before he tired so badly that he had to stop. "I thought, 'That's pitiful,'" Tom says. "I was only thirty-eight, and I could only run a block. I thought that I should be able to go at least a mile. I was playing volleyball twice a week and had kidded myself that this meant that I was fit. I was upset about finding out I was in such terrible shape."

So the next morning, Tom, with Cinnamon in tow, ran a little longer than a block. Every day, he walked the dog, and every day, he added to the previous day's distance run. His goal was to run a mile without stopping. Interestingly, Cinnamon knew about Tom's new work ethic before his wife, Jill, did. "One of my neighbors saw me running," Tom relates, "and then said to Jill matter of factly, 'I saw Tom running.' That was the first she knew of it. I hadn't told her because I didn't want to eat crow if I didn't stick with it."

But he did, and was able to run a mile within 3 weeks. Already, he had lost 10 pounds. "That was a big motivation to keep going," Tom says. "I also wanted to see how much I could build up to run comfortably." After 6 months, he was up to 4 miles a day, always with Cinnamon. After 9 months, he had lost 40 pounds. (Cinnamon, a half Labrador retriever/half golden retriever, "is still fat," Tom reports.) Tom's resting pulse, which had been in the high 70s, was down to 57.

Tom also realized less quantifiable, but just as significant, benefits. As a manager of stores for an optometry chain and the father of two preteens, "my butt used to be dragging around by dinnertime," he says. "Now, I'm more energetic all the way around, even though I go to bed after midnight and get up at 6 A.M. to run. It's a great way to start the day—I feel so awake the rest of the day, and it gives me time to reflect on things."

Tom now runs 3 miles a day at about 10 minutes per mile. "I used to think about wanting to go farther or faster," he says, "but I'm very comfortable with my routine." And why shouldn't he be? He's a perfect example of how you can revolutionize your life with just a bit of perseverance and a minor investment of time. "I never think about stopping running,"

Tom says. "So much of my life has improved, and with only a half hour a day.

"I wish I had discovered this ten years ago," he adds. "If someone had told me in high school that twenty years later I'd be running three miles a day and liking it, I would have told him he was crazy."

Getting Fit

STEPS ON THE PATH TO LIFETIME FITNESS

If you keep your running simple, you can more easily incorporate it into your life on a regular basis. I emphasize an intelligent approach that works for you that you know you can sustain.

One of the things I most want to get across in this book is that running should be simple. You don't need tons of special equipment, manicured playing fields or 10 other people to do it. A lot of fancy accouterments have been invented that are supposed to make running easier, such as heart rate monitors, multifunction watches and computer-based training programs, and they can be helpful. But they're not fundamental. I believe that if you keep your running simple, it will consistently be more enjoyable, and you can more easily incorporate it into your life on a regular basis.

So I'm not going to get into a detailed discussion of every gadget and piece of gear that's out there for runners. (If you're interested, all of the major running magazines do a good job of evaluating these items.) Instead, I want to focus on four topics—shoes, apparel, diet and record keeping—that nearly all runners are interested in, and that all runners should pay attention to. These four matters might not seem to have much in common, but they do: you can greatly increase the enjoyment of your running by tending to them intelligently, and with each, there's no universal approach that's best for all runners. With shoes, clothing, diet and logs, it's likely you'll spend your life as a runner experimenting, discarding what doesn't work for you, trying new approaches that a runner you respect recommends, and tweaking old practices as age and circumstance change the emphases of your running.

SHOES

In the early '70s, when I was training very hard but had yet to break through to the world-class level, I tried to get as much as I could out of my running shoes. After all, they cost a lot of money given how much I was making. Plus, in those days, nobody talked about midsole compression, uneven sole wear or many of the other things that happen to shoes after you've done a lot of running in them. So I just wore them until they were destroyed.

Around 1973, I was having trouble with a strain in my calf muscle. I went to see a trainer about the problem. He put his hand in my shoe and said, "Well, no wonder—there's no arch support in here anymore." The shoe was totally flattened; it was practically falling off of my feet! The trainer convinced me that I needed new shoes, and ever since then, I've been much more mindful of how important good running shoes are.

Basics of Shoe Selection

I'm often asked, "What's the best running shoe?" That's an unanswerable question. A better one is, "What's the best running shoe *for me*?" I weigh about 130 pounds and land with the most force on my forefeet. The shoes that are best for me are very different from those for someone who, for example, weighs 185 pounds and is a heavy heel striker.

The first step is to determine how you run. Are you an overpronator? That is, do your feet roll in more than they should when they land? Maybe you're a supinator, like I am, meaning that you tend to land on the outside of your feet and not roll in enough as you push off. Or maybe you have a "normal" footstrike, in which you land on the outside of your feet, then roll in a bit as you push off. These three basic types of footstrike require different configurations of the standard features of a running shoe. I can't give hard and fast rules to help you determine which type of footstrike you have; it's best to have someone at a specialty running store or an experienced runner who you know help.

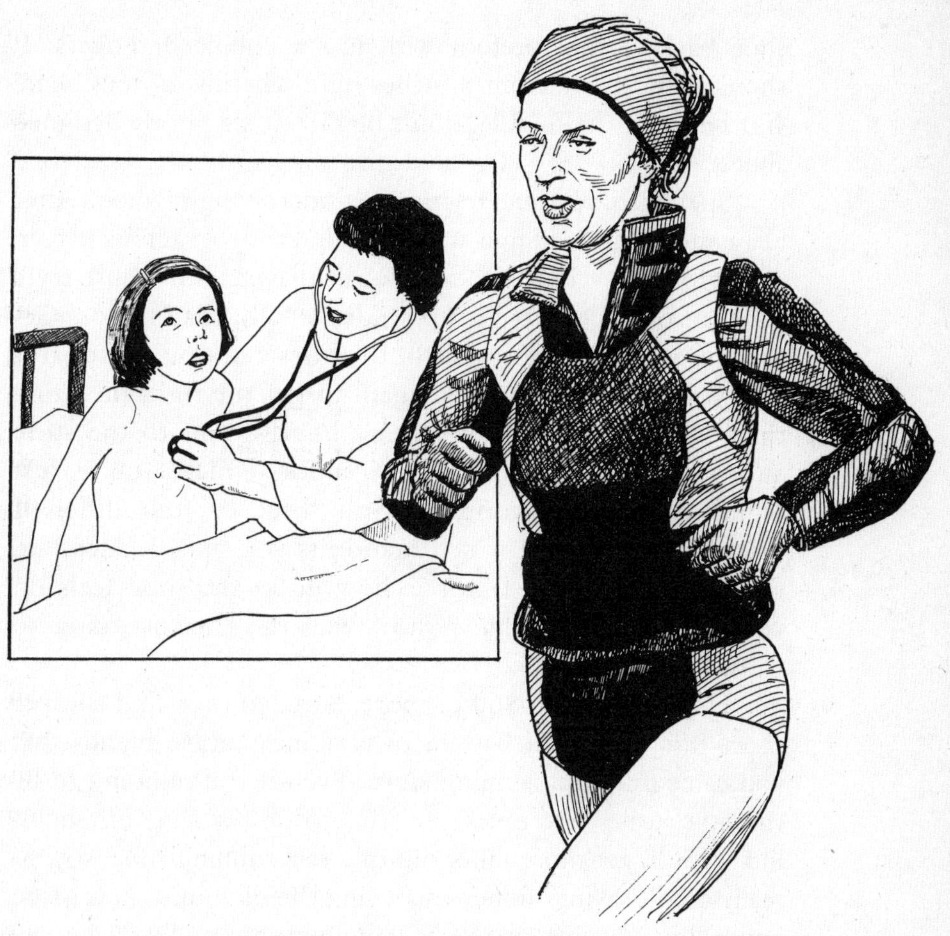

No matter what type of footstrike you have, the most important feature of a running shoe is its fit. It can't be too tight or too loose; your feet have to feel good within the shoe. Most people do best with a good balance of features: look for a firm heel counter to provide stability, but it should also be flexible in the forefoot. Obviously, you want the shoe to have good cushioning, but not too much. If the shoe has too much cushioning, it might lack flexibility in the forefoot, and this can cause you to get tight calf muscles, leading to plantar fasciitis, shin splints or some other injury. That's not what you want from a shoe! You should be able to push the shoe back at the forefoot with just a couple of fingers. It should bend back about 3 inches right where your toes bend. If it bends at the middle, don't buy it—it's a poorly designed shoe.

Spend some time trying to find the right shoe. After all, a shoe is to a runner what a racquet is to a tennis player, or a glove or a bat is to a baseball player. Don't just try a shoe on one foot, lace it up and say, "Oh, that's fine." Get up and move around with both shoes on; you'll probably find you need to lace them again to get the right fit. Bring the socks that you'll be running in with you to the store and wear them as you try on shoes. Unless you're just replacing an old favorite, try on three or four different models to determine which brand fits you best. Remember, the most important factor is how good the shoe feels on your foot; what counts is how well the shoe is going to work for you.

Expect to spend $60 or more. Sure, you can find cheaper shoes out there, but beware of very inexpensive brands that you can't find in a running store. Even if you're going to be running just a few miles at a time, don't scrimp on shoes. First, you'll get more miles out of a real running shoe, so you really aren't saving money by buying the discount ones. More important, you have to treat your body right. You'll be less sore and will enjoy your running more if you spend the little bit of extra money for high-quality shoes.

Of course, there are also shoes at the other extreme that cost a small fortune and seem to incorporate every technology of the last 20 years. Many of these shoes have more to do with marketing hype than with helping you run better. Traditionally, athletes have had little impact on shoe design, and based on what I see out there, that's still the case. The tendency over the past few years has been to make running shoes too heavy, too inflexible and too, well, too much—giant, flared heels, giant cushioning units under the heel, even computers in the heel! How much do we really need these things? Despite the use of lightweight materials, so many running shoes weigh 12 ounces or more. What are we supposed to do in them, go hiking? Fortunately, most companies offer solid, middle of the road shoes that have all the features you need for around $60 or $70.

Where should you buy your shoes? You can't beat a specialty running shop for selection and knowledgeable staff. They should let you do as much walking and running as you want in shoes you are thinking about buying. Find out from runners the stores that can be trusted in your area. If you're a beginner and don't know many other runners, find a store that has a selection of at least three or four well-known brands. The more shoes you can choose from, the more likely it is you'll find a manufacturer whose shoes work best for you.

When to Switch and Ditch Shoes

Watch the wear and tear on your shoes. You'll be able to tell when they're really starting to wear down—they'll feel lighter, the midsole will likely have wrinkles in it as it becomes more compressed, one layer of the outsole might be worn away, and the heel counter might be tilting in. After awhile, you won't even need to look at your shoes to know when it's time to stop running in them. You'll start to feel more sore than usual from your training, or you'll notice little things, such as landing on a rock and having it really hurt because your shoe has lost so much cushioning.

There comes a point where you're asking for trouble if you keep running in shoes that are too worn down. You might think you're saving money by making the shoes last longer, but you'll likely spend that money on doctor bills, X rays and rehab because of getting injured. And that's not to mention the diminished enjoyment you'll get from your running because your shoes are causing you soreness or pain. The name of the game is avoiding injury. Don't make the mistakes that I used to; it just isn't worth it.

Shoe Doctoring

Most people, including me, find that they can get 500–600 miles out of a pair of high-quality shoes. There are some things you can do to maximize how long your shoes serve you well. For example, I have a little area on the forefoot of my left shoe that wears down long before the rest of either shoe. I can sometimes get another 2 or 3 weeks out of a pair of shoes if I apply Shoe Goo to this spot every 2 or 3 days. After I do that, I'm back to normal biomechanically. That is, the wear on my shoes isn't making me run differently; my footstrike is back to how it should be.

You can also extend the life of a shoe by doctoring the inside. I think most of the arch supports and inserts that come with running shoes are very weak. They're insubstantial, and they don't have much effect in terms of supporting you laterally under the arch. I would like to see shoe companies beef up the inserts that go in shoes, especially as the running population continues to get older.

Until that happens, it's up to you. As your shoes get a bit worn, you can take out the standard-issue insert and replace it with one of the many commercial inserts that are available at running stores. Many of these supply extra cushioning, which I find to be helpful as the midsoles of my shoes compress. Heel lifts can also be helpful if you're battling a case of Achilles tendinitis.

If you continually get injured in the same spots, especially on the same side of your body, you might need prescription orthotics. Some people may have some sort of structural problem, such as one leg being longer than the other, that is

going to affect how they feel if they do any real amount of running. A podiatrist or physical therapist can perform a biomechanical evaluation of how you run, then devise a mold to place inside your shoes that will help you counter these problems.

In general, though, you shouldn't have to make many alterations to your shoes. Don't get orthotics, for example, just because one person tells you to. Keep running simple. It's tempting to think that all of your injuries have a readily diagnosable medical explanation, because then they seem easier to fix. But we're a society of excess, and we tend to overprescribe devices instead of looking for the simplest cure. Injury is often the result of something more basic, such as your shoes wearing down or you overdoing it and your body breaking down just a bit.

Young Runners' Shoes

Children often think they can get away with running in shoes that are made for other sports. They usually don't know any better, and if their parents aren't runners, their parents might be reluctant to spend $60 or more for something that the children might lose interest in after a week.

Still, young runners need good running shoes just like anybody else. I often read about teenage runners getting injured, and it's no surprise why: their bones are still developing, and the tendons and ligaments in their legs might not be ready to bear the load of too much running. Often, their energy and enthusiasm are greater than their ability, and they tend to train too much, too fast. Young runners should buy running shoes that have plenty of cushioning to help counter some of the factors working against them. Why start a running career with injury? That's no way to instill a lifelong interest in the sport.

Older Runners' Shoes

When I turned 40, there were no more good shoes. Nothing seemed to work right or feel right: my shoes felt heavier, my training seemed harder, and I just felt so tired all the time. Mother Nature was the same, the roads were the same, but I had changed.

Many masters runners have this experience. You lose some of the fat pads in the bottoms of your feet with age, so the same amount of cushioning in a shoe that might have been enough 10 years ago no longer seems adequate. Also, it's likely that your muscles, tendons and ligaments aren't as strong and resilient as they used to be, so your legs feel the thousands of footsteps you take on every run that much more. I use cushioned inserts in my shoes more and more as I get older. It's also important to consider what you put your shoes on as well as what you put in them. Run on even dirt and grass when you can; doing so is less wear and tear on your shoes and on you.

Racing Shoes

Twenty years ago, almost all of the racing shoes were made for runners like me—light and fast. As more people of more sizes and speeds became runners, they tended to keep that view and think that they shouldn't wear racing shoes. I think that's wrong. Today, in addition to many "pure" racing flats (minimalist models that weigh 7 ounces or less), there is a good selection of lightweight training shoes (around 9 ounces or so). These shoes are light enough to feel different when you want to run hard, but supportive and substantial enough to protect you from injury. There's nothing like lacing up a pair of lighter shoes than you're used to training in to get you psyched up for a fast run. If you're going to wear different shoes for racing, then do some of your training, especially your faster running, in them. This will prepare your tendons and ligaments for when you race in them, and you'll not be as sore and beat up afterward.

RUNNING APPAREL

As with shoes, the most important factors to consider in choosing running apparel are fit and function. You should always be thinking in terms of how to make your running easier; with apparel, this means your physical comfort. You don't want clothes that are going to chafe, that are not going to breathe, or that are going to cling to your skin as you start to sweat.

Learn how to make different fabrics work for you, both by themselves and, when it's cold, in combination with other fabrics. First, let's consider warm weather running. Many runners, especially beginners, overdress when they run. Even with some experience, it's easy to forget just how much heat you can create while running—some people produce 11 times the amount of heat when they're running than they do when they're at rest. That means that even in what seems like moderate weather, if you're in doubt about whether you need a piece of clothing, leave it off. After just a few minutes, you can be very comfortable running in a T-shirt and shorts when the temperature is in the 50s. Most Americans have no regular connection to the outdoors, though, so they don't really know how 55 degrees compares to 65 degrees compares to 45 degrees. When they start running, they wear too much, and that's only going to make that difficult beginning phase of running that much harder.

A cotton T-shirt is the standard, as you've no doubt noticed if you attend any road race. Many times, that's all you need, but for around $20, you can get shirts made of Cool-

Max or other light fabrics that do a much better job of removing the moisture you generate as you heat up. This not only helps you stay cooler, but you'll just feel better if your shirt isn't soaked and clinging to you. The same fabrics are available as singlets for when it's 70 degrees or warmer, and when it gets much above 80 degrees, many men will run with no shirt, and some women will run wearing only a running bra. Warm weather running is pretty much a no-brainer—wear as little as you can to stay as cool as you can.

Things get trickier when the weather gets nastier. Here's where running gear shares another similarity with running shoes—some of the high-tech gear can be quite expensive, and you might be tempted to try to get by with cheapies. This is especially the case for beginners who aren't sure if they are going to stick with it in the winter and who don't know enough about performance fabrics to believe that they can really make a difference. Trust me—a good running suit beats a department store pair of sweats any day. I've run in all those old, heavy garments, and I know what a difference good gear makes. You always want to be thinking in terms of making your running easier; when cold weather becomes a big adversary, the right apparel is often the difference between enjoying a run and hating it.

By now, most people have heard about layering—that a few light layers are better than one heavy one at keeping you warm and comfortable during winter workouts. That's because layers trap the warmth your body generates on the run while allowing moisture and excess heat to move to the surface and dissipate. Light layers also allow greater freedom of movement, not to mention convenience: as conditions merit, you can remove them.

What many people haven't heard is what those layers should consist of. Three cotton shirts, for example, meet the several-light-layers criterion, but they won't keep you dry once you've started sweating or if it's raining or snowing.

Each layer has a purpose, and different fabrics are made to meet the requirements of each.

The layer closest to your skin should wick moisture to the next layer. Even in very cold weather, you sweat; if this moisture stays near your skin, you'll not only feel uncomfortable, but you'll also risk losing too much warmth. Polypropylene is one of the best-known examples of a base layer fabric. Most of the apparel companies have special names for their own version of a base layer fabric, but they're all pretty much the same. You want to look for dual-channel fabrics. These have a hydrophobic, or water-hating, layer next to your skin and a hydrophilic, or water-loving, layer on the outside; this construction moves moisture away from your skin before you start to feel clammy. In moderate winter weather—say, 40 degrees, low wind and no precipitation—these garments can suffice as your only layer. Tights and tops of these types of fabrics will cost about $40 apiece.

When the conditions are worse, you want to add an outer layer that will block snow, wind and rain while allowing sweat to continue moving away from your skin. For years, the standard setter in this category was Gore-Tex. Its construction allowed sweat vapor to pass through to the outside, but wouldn't allow moisture to get in, all the while blocking the wind. Several fabrics now exist, such as Windstopper, Activent and ThinTech, that achieve these purposes while being quieter, more breathable, lighter and better feeling than Gore-Tex. Expect to pay more than $100 for a good suit.

Often, the combination of moisture-wicking base layer with a windproof, water-resistant outer shell will do the job. In severe conditions, however, an intermediate layer will act as insulator. Garments of this layer should be warm and have many of the wicking properties of your internal layer.

Given the investment involved in garments like these, you're better off buying them at a running store where you can feel the fabrics, try on the garments, and so on.

DIET

Too much importance is placed on the runner's diet. That's not to say it's not important, just that it should be kept in perspective. I meet many runners who think eating x amount of y nutrient is the key to running well. Often these runners, who are so meticulous about tracking every morsel that goes in their mouths, consistently neglect major parts of a well-rounded training program, such as regular long runs. It's as if they think that they can eat themselves to a personal record, and bypass the steady, hard work that running good races requires.

A moderate approach to diet is the most sustainable in the long run. Some people think that being a runner means living on nuts and berries. Yes, running often makes you more conscious about eating healthfully, and if you're training to race well, there's plenty of benefit to be had from paying attention to your diet. But that doesn't mean you have to go overboard. I can't count the number of times I've been asked incredulously, "You drink coffee?" It's as if nonrunners think we've chosen not to enjoy life when, in fact, we're likely to be enjoying it more than they are. There was a Nike ad a few years ago that showed a man sitting comfortably inside a restaurant sipping a brandy and looking with bewilderment at a runner darting past the window on a dark, rainy night. I know people who got into discussions about which of the two people in the ad they'd rather be. To me, it's a silly discussion—as runners, we live life more fully, and can be both of the people. We'll enjoy that warm meal in the cozy restaurant all that much more after putting in a solid effort. Who says the runner in that ad had to go home and chomp on a few rice cakes?

My point is that the runner's diet should not be fundamentally different from what we know should be everybody's diet—high in carbohydrate (55 to 65 percent of calories), low in fat (15 to 25 percent of calories), with adequate calories, protein, vitamins and minerals to allow your body to get the most out of your training. Up to a certain level, there's no difference between eating for health and eating for performance. Eat at least five servings of fruits and vegetables a day, watch your intake of animal fat (no more than 10 percent of your calories should come from saturated fat), get plenty of fiber—by now, these guidelines are pretty much common sense. As with training consistently, though, the hard part isn't discovering the basics, but sticking to them reasonably well for months and years at a time.

So instead of pretending that I have some great dietary secrets to impart, I'll focus on a few matters concerning diet that have had increased pertinence to me since I've become a masters runner.

Culinary Corrections

I don't regret much of what I did when I was trying to be the best in the world, but, in retrospect, I wish I had eaten better. Let's just say that if I knew in 1977 what I know now about the benefits of proper nutrition, a certain manufacturer of mayonnaise would have lost a lot of business. These essential truths hit home much harder when you're older. You can get away with recuperative and nutritional murder in your youth, but the onset of age requires employing every possible advantage to keep yourself physically afloat.

Thanks to humorous descriptions of my eating habits in some of the running magazines, I acquired the moniker, "King of Junk Food" as well as "King of the Road." I'd like to set the record straight. I did not eat junk food; I ate weird food. For example, I would often come in from a hard training run and down a jar of pickle juice or a big swig from the maple syrup bottle. It seems that more people knew that I sometimes put mayonnaise on my pizza crust than knew what

I could run for 10K. Some of my favorite meals included just about anything with peanut butter, mayonnaise, horseradish or soy sauce dumped all over it.

Why did I change how I eat? Perhaps it was the horrified looks from my family when I would sit down to a bowl of cereal with all of the above condiments on it. Or perhaps it was discovering that after all the years of training, my cholesterol levels still hovered in the mid-200s. Or perhaps it was finally realizing that a better diet just made me feel markedly better in my running.

Whatever the reason, there have been permanent changes in the contents of my pantry and refrigerator. I eat more fruit and vegetables than I used to, I'm more careful about how food is prepared (to ensure that it's not too fatty) and I take advantage of the many good reduced- or nonfat foods now available, such as peanut butter and salad dressing.

But I haven't become perfect. Occasionally, if I'm visiting someone who has good mayonnaise on hand, I'll indulge a little. Man does not live on bread alone, after all.

Water, Water Nowhere?

One of the most important things that you can do to help your running seems so simple and obvious, but for some reason, most of us find it hard to incorporate in our daily routines. Nearly all of us should drink more water. It seems our sense of thirst isn't as in tune as it should be. This is especially true for masters runners; with age, your thirst mechanism becomes even less efficient, and many older runners are so busy at work all day that they never think about stopping for a drink of water.

I think most runners, myself included, have walked around for years in a state of semi-dehydration. If I make myself drink water whether I'm thirsty or not, I notice a benefit in my running and recovery. Feeling absolutely terrible in many races, including the seven hot, humid marathons that I've dropped out of, was, I believe, the result of not drinking enough water before and during the events. I don't know why it's such a hard thing to do, except that eating is fun, and drinking water is not.

Different Dietary Needs of Masters Runners

Should masters runners take any special dietary steps? There hasn't been much research on how the nutritional needs of older athletes differ from those of younger active people. Also, most of the advice given about eating for older adults assumes that people are sedentary. The evidence, then, is incomplete, but here's what sports nutritionists advise masters runners to pay special attention to in their diets:

FLUIDS: As I said, it's tough for masters runners to stay adequately hydrated. Our thirst mechanism, which does a poor enough job of signaling our needs at any age, becomes even less sensitive as we get older. There are also changes in kidney function with age that complicate the matter. Then there's a double whammy—compared to younger athletes, masters have higher core body temperatures, heart rates and overall loss of body water in response to heat. In other words, not only is it likely that we're starting a training run or race less hydrated than younger runners, but once out there, the weather takes that much more out of us! I can't overemphasize the importance of always being well-hydrated. This is true for all runners, but masters runners need to be especially careful about it. Drink, drink, drink. You should urinate frequently during the day, and your urine should be clear-colored.

CALORIES: I weigh pretty much what I did 20 years ago. I realize that I'm not average, but there's usually no good reason to weigh 20 pounds more at age 55 than you did at age 30. After all, it's probably not 20 pounds of muscle you gained. That extra weight will obviously slow you down, as well as increase your risk of injury owing to the extra pounding. Running performance aside, your risks for many degenerative diseases, including cancer and heart disease, are greater when you put on too much fat.

Aging causes your body's metabolic rate to decrease and your tendency to gain weight to increase. (You probably didn't need me to tell you this!) Even if your weight stays the same over the years, it's likely that you've put on some fat, because with age we lose muscle mass. Many older runners who are trying to watch their weight actually make things worse by too severely restricting their calories. When you do this, your metabolism slows down that much more, and you might lose even more muscle. When you're a masters runner, you need all the muscle you can get!

The good news is that running allows you to eat more calories than your sedentary contemporaries. This makes it easier to ensure that you're eating enough to get a good, balanced diet, which can be hard for sedentary folks.

PROTEIN: Your stomach produces less acid as you get older; this reduces your ability to digest protein, and it may affect absorption of vitamin B–12. Most people find they prefer to eat less animal protein as they get older. Although this isn't bad in itself, it does mean you should be more careful about getting adequate protein from nonmeat sources. Unless it's balanced by complementary proteins from grains, cereals and vegetables, a diet that's low in animal products—particularly lean red meat—incurs the risk of anemia and other ailments that will curtail your running.

CALCIUM: After menopause, women need to increase their calcium intake from 1,000mg per day to 1,500mg. Otherwise, they're at an increased risk for osteoporosis. Although women runners have an advantage over sedentary older women because running and other weight-bearing exercises increase bone mineral density, they still need to be mindful of this; the same weight-bearing nature of running makes less dense bones more susceptible to stress fractures. Calcium is most effectively absorbed in the presence of dairy products, so even if you're getting some of your calcium through other means, such as calcium supplements, eat or drink dairy products when taking them. Here's one area in which runners' ability to eat more than sedentary people really pays off, because it can be tough to eat enough of the right foods to get 1,500mg of calcium a day if you're sedentary and have a diminished appetite. See the attached chart for top sources of calcium.

VITAMIN D: Aging decreases your skin's ability to produce vitamin D. Many older runners, myself included, are rightfully concerned about skin cancer and wear sunscreen. Also, older runners are likely to find themselves running at nonpeak sun hours because of work and family responsibilities. All of this means that masters runners should take extra steps to get adequate amounts of vitamin D, which works with calcium to keep your bones strong. Fortified nonfat milk is the best source.

Sources of Calcium—Dairy's Queen

400MG PER SERVING

8 ounces plain lowfat or nonfat yogurt
4 ounces tofu processed with calcium salts
3.5 ounces sardines with the bones

300MG PER SERVING

1 cup skim, lowfat or whole milk, or lowfat chocolate milk

1 cup buttermilk
8 ounces plain whole milk yogurt
½ cup part-skim ricotta cheese
¼ cup instant nonfat powdered milk
1 cup cooked, drained collard greens (from frozen)

200MG PER SERVING

1 ounce cheese (cheddar, part-skim mozzarella, muenster, provolone, pasteurized or processed American, or Swiss)
1 cup ice cream or ice milk
3.5 ounces canned pink salmon with the bones
1 cup cooked, drained kale (from raw or frozen)
1 cup cooked, drained turnip greens (from raw or frozen)

100MG PER SERVING

¾ cup lowfat or creamed cottage cheese
1 cup cooked, drained broccoli (from frozen)
1⅓ cups cooked, drained broccoli (from raw)
¾ cup cooked, drained collard greens (from raw)
1 cup cooked, drained kale (from raw)
1 cup cooked, drained Northern, navy or pinto beans

RECORD KEEPING

Here's a random page out of one of my favorite books: "A.M.: 15 miles, cool, tired, rained, nice wind; P.M.: rest."

Yes, that's an entry for one day from my training log. Many runners, especially those who are working toward a goal, track their training like this, and they often write more than I do. I've never kept very extensive records; for example, I couldn't look in my log and tell you how many miles I ran last year without doing a lot of arithmetic. I record my weekly mileage, and I track it as a week progresses, but that's it. As

I've said before, I like to keep running simple. Entries like the above are sufficient to get a sense of how my training is going.

Looking to the Past

That doesn't mean you should just copy my format, or that there's no value in keeping more extensive records than I do. Your training log is kind of your running diary—it should contain references to anything that might have had an impact on your running on a given day, and it can be as detailed or cryptic as you want.

For me, that means that in addition to my mileage for the day, I write about any significant weather. You might feel like you're dragging in your training and not know why, then look in your log and realize that for 5 of the last 6 days you've written something like, "Hot. Tired. Struggled." Or maybe you spent your run battling a headwind that threw you off. It's very important to keep those things in mind in your training—how much is Mother Nature affecting you? Usually, this means tracking bad weather, but I like to note the nice days, too, like one of the first warm days of spring when you can't help but feel good on your run.

I also write down anything that's happening in my professional or family life that might affect my running. I sometimes feel like I'm always going to or coming from an airport, and traveling so much can be tough on your training. So I always note when I flew somewhere, or if I'm still feeling jet-lagged, or if I didn't get enough sleep because of my children being sick. There are always reasons for the way you feel, and your log can help you discern them.

What I did in my training that day is another of the factors I regularly track. If I do a speed workout, I'll write down my number of hard repeats, what kind of rest interval I took between them, and how fast I ran them. Or if I run a course with two big hills in it, I'll write, "10 miles. 2 big hills." And if I do any crosstraining, such as weights or swimming, I'll write these down. I don't record my pulse, and I've never kept track of my weight in my log, except occasionally in the heat, when doing so is a good way for me to keep on top of staying hydrated.

Looking to the Future

I also use my log as record keeping for my racing. It's very valuable to track your progress as you move toward a goal. I especially like to compare how I'm currently doing to previous years.

For example, if I'm pointing toward the Bix 7-miler, which is a race I run nearly every year, I like to be able to see what I ran there when I was 42, and how my training is going for it more than 5 years later. How much and what kind of speed work was I doing then? How does that compare to now? I might be able to see that I'm hurting a bit in a certain area of my training. Or I might look at it and gain a great deal of confidence: here is the visible manifestation of my training. Many runners lack confidence in themselves and their abilities, and they can look to their log to gain some. (I suppose that includes me, because I still keep one after all of these years!)

Again, you don't have to follow my format. Say you're a beginning runner and you want to lose 30 pounds. Track your weight in your log. That's a goal that you can mark progress to, just like focusing on a certain race and trying to reach a certain level of fitness for it is a goal for me. The same thing applies if you've been running a few miles a day and want to try to run more. Write down with pride when you run farther than you have before so you have a record of the great strides you're making.

Potential Dangers of a Log

Mileage is the key to success in distance running. Up to a point, the more you run, the better you run.

But there's a strong temptation to look at your log and say, "Well, I hit this number of miles last week, so this week I have to do at least that many, if not more." That's a mistake. Even when I was training to try to be the best marathoner in the world, and was meticulous about tracking my weekly mileage, I was sure to let what I saw in my log reflect my training, not dictate it.

That danger—of losing sight of why you're doing what you're doing—is there for everybody. Your log should be a tool to keep these counterproductive, obsessive impulses under control. If you keep accurate records of how you feel in your training, your log can help you answer this fundamental question: Am I training smart, or am I not thinking about it and just doing certain types of training to help my log look better?

Getting Fast

THE HOWS AND WHYS OF RACING

I want to encourage as many people as possible to attend races regularly, because doing so adds so much to your enjoyment of the sport, and makes it more likely that you'll stick with it for a lifetime. Once you've experienced racing, you'll understand that there's a kind of fun that comes from challenging yourself within very sharply defined parameters.

One of my first runs was in gym class. I ran the fastest time of anyone in the school, so immediately I thought that competition would be important and gratifying. I still do. Good health, peace of mind, being outdoors, camaraderie—these are all wonderful things that come to you when you run. But for me, the real pull of running—the proverbial icing on the cake—has always been racing. The nature of racing is one of the things that separates our sport from most others—it's about unadulterated human performance. In other sports, you're maneuvering against your opponents, trying to knock them down, trying to finesse some piece of equipment. Not so in running. Ultimately, it's just you and the elements. In some respects, because it's more simple, it's more complex.

There are many approaches to training for racing and for running races. For most runners, their main opponents are themselves. You're out there to see how much of your potential you can attain on a given day, taking into account your training, the weather, the terrain, etc. So don't think what I have to say in this chapter applies only to people who are trying to win their age groups or get under a certain time in the marathon. I want to encourage as many people as possible to attend races regularly, because doing so adds so much to your enjoyment of the sport, and makes it more likely you'll stick with it for a lifetime. So in our look at how to train for races and what strategies to use in races, I'm going to talk in general terms that almost any runner can apply to his or her situation.

WHY RACE?

Whenever I'm asked what's so great about racing, my immediate response is that it's fun. Most people who haven't tried it can't believe this. They think that running is synonymous with drudgery, and that the only way to have fun is to be entertained by someone else. Once you've experienced racing, though, you understand that there's a kind of fun that comes from challenging yourself within very sharply defined parameters. I don't want to make too much of this, but there aren't many opportunities in our society to face such primal challenges, where it's just you and your mind and your body trying to reach your physical potential.

I'm fortunate enough to be able to break records, first in the open division and now in different age groups. That's a great thrill to me, because I love exploring new territory, and it's exciting to think I've done something that no one has before. But you don't have to be a record breaker to get the same excitement and sense of challenge out of your running. One of the keys to our sport is that there are a million ways to define success. Like I said, most runners' main opponents are themselves—running faster than you have for a certain distance, running farther than you have, seeing how close you can get to times you ran 10 years ago, and so on. To me, that's the nitty gritty. You get to define what your standards of success are, and then you have an objective way to assess your performance. Plus, if you race frequently, you have a way to track your progress and see whether you're improving. You're being rewarded for your efforts. That's much harder to do in other sports, where teammates or equipment or judges' rulings or some other outside force makes determining how you're doing so much more subjective.

It's also hard to get that sense of measurable success in the other parts of your life. Maybe you're good at your job, but you get passed over for a promotion because someone

else is better at schmoozing. And how do you get tangible feedback of your efforts at being a good spouse or parent? There's none of that in racing. You put out an effort, and you get a black and white record of how you did. It doesn't matter who you know or how well you dress or any of the other things that influence success in other parts of your life.

That's not to say that races aren't fun in the more conventional sense. If you've never been to a road race, then perhaps you'll more readily believe one of the major myths about our sport—that runners don't smile. Just about everyone I see at road races is smiling, laughing and sharing their experiences. A road race is the closest thing to a party I can think of. There's music, food, good will and positive energy. Yes, during a race most of the competitors aren't smiling. I guess some people want us to be smiling all the time. But the great fun of the post-race scene is due in large part to the runners feeling of accomplishment after the race. They've worked hard, and having been to the edge of their potential on that day, the chance to relax and socialize with similar people is that much more enjoyable.

This side of racing can open it up to so many runners who mistakenly think that all racers are record-conscious whippets like me. At a race during the summer of 1995, I met a woman who had been a state champion in cross country in high school. She didn't do as well in college, got burnt out and frustrated and swore off racing. A few years later, she realized she missed the social aspect of races, and she started attending low-key club races. When I talked with her, she almost seemed embarrassed about liking these and not really caring about her times. I told her that she has nothing to apologize for. You should always be evaluating your running. If you realize that you want to shift gears and emphasize other sides of the sport, that's fine. Your running should be only for you, and if you're comfortable with where you are, that's all that matters.

I certainly have my phases when I don't feel like racing, especially in the summer when running can be a struggle from the first step. And someday I may retire from competition. I used to be a marathoner, but I'm not anymore. In the same way, I've been a competition-oriented runner since I was 15, but I can see where that might change down the road if the wear and tear of all those years of hard training gets to me, and I can't perform at the level that I want. But even then, I'll always attend races, and revel in the great fun of all those runners out there helping each other reach their varied goals.

FINDING YOUR BEST RACE DISTANCE

I learned early on that I'm not a sprinter. During high school and college, I raced the half-mile, mile and 2-mile. Although I did reasonably well at these distances—I was very proud when I broke 9:00 for 2 miles in college—I always felt limited while racing them. Once I was exposed to longer road races in college, I discovered why. I'm a long distance runner; to be more specific, I'm a marathoner. That doesn't mean I can't run well at other distances, especially if I focus on them, but the marathon is the event for which I'm best physically and psychologically suited.

There's a perfect race distance out there for you, too. Finding what it is shouldn't require too much guessing. I lack sprint speed and explosive power, but I've always been able to maintain a moderately hard effort for a long time. Also, mentally I can handle a lot of boredom, at least if I've chosen to put myself in that situation. That is, I have a high threshold for tedium if I know there's a point to it. Biomechanically, I'm efficient—I don't crash into the ground every time my foot hits the ground, and I don't waste energy with up and down movements when I run. Finally, I was blessed with strong connective tissues, so when I was younger I could regularly run 130–150 miles a week, as you must to succeed internationally in the marathon, and not get injured. Put these elements together, and you've got a marathoner.

To find out your best race distance, think about the types of workouts that you most enjoy doing and are best at. There aren't cut and dry rules, but you can get some general ideas this way. Do you like pushing the pace for a half hour run, but get really bored with 90-minute runs? Then you're more of a middle distance road racer—you'll probably do best at 5-milers and shorter. Can you handle long runs, but most enjoy those regular medium effort runs of an hour or so? Then you're probably best suited to races in the 10-mile to half marathon range. And if you feel as if it takes you 5 miles just to get going, and you seem to get stronger as a long run progresses while your training partners get increasingly tired, it's probably a safe bet you're well-suited for the marathon. Again, these are generalizations, but I think you race best at the distances that best suit your psyche.

Of course, you can train yourself to shift gears mentally. Marathoners can do speed workouts of short repeats and learn to tolerate better the sharp pain that accompanies anaerobic running; this will help them better attack a 5K from the start and come closer to their potential. Conversely, short distance specialists can learn how to tolerate the more subtle discomfort of longer races and the ability to ration their resources over a longer time with more long runs and speed workouts of longer repeats, such as mile intervals.

Your physiology also plays a big part in determining your best distance. It's likely that it coincides with the type of workout you most enjoy. Like I said, I lack explosive power. In physiological terms, this is because a high percentage of my muscles are made of slow-twitch fibers. These contract relatively slowly, but they can keep doing so for a long time as long as they're fueled. I have a lower-than-normal percentage of fast-twitch fibers, which contract very rapidly, but fatigue quickly. For me, this translates to the ability to run close to my maximum at a given distance for a long time, and the inability to produce one effort at that distance that's significantly faster. When I used to do track workouts with the Greater Boston Track Club, some of the guys would get to the end of the workout and run their last one or two repeats faster than what they had been averaging by 10 seconds or more. I can't do that. At my best, I would run workouts of 8 half-miles in just over 2:10, but I've never broken 2:00 for a single half-mile in my life. I'm sure I could have had I targeted my training more toward that goal, but I don't think I would have gotten too far under.

Think about your abilities in this way. You don't even have to use examples from your running to assess your physiological makeup. Say you've done some weight lifting. If you have the ability to produce one all-out bench press that's noticeably heavier than the weight that you can lift for 10 repetitions, you're toward the fast-twitch side of things. If you can do 10 repetitions at 100 pounds, but really struggle to do one at 120 pounds, you're probably more of a long distance runner. There are other factors involved, I know, but looking at these types of abilities can help you get started in finding your best distance.

If you've already done a lot of racing, compare your PRs using the table of equal performances in this book's appendix. It's likely that you'll find a range of distances in which your PRs are noticeably superior to those at other distances. Because his PRs fall within those listed in the chart, I'll use my coauthor, Scott Douglas, as an example. Scott has run 30:48 for 10K and 51:01 for 10 miles. Extrapolating from the chart, these are equivalent performances. The same level of performances at shorter distances would produce a mile time of 4:11–4:12, and a 2-mile of just under 9:10. But Scott's bests at those distances are 4:28 and 9:31, and there's even discrepancy between these two marks. When based on his 2-mile time, Scott's mile time is still relatively slow, because his 9:31 2-mile equates to a 4:22 or so mile. At the other end of the spectrum, Scott's 10K time should yield a 2:27 marathon; Scott's best is only 2:43.

This makes sense. Scott has even less explosive power than I do—he's never broken 60 seconds for a quarter mile, which most mediocre high school runners can do, and his vertical leap is only 11 inches, so his performances become relatively less impressive the shorter the race becomes. Scott bounces when he runs, and although this form problem is a hindrance at all distances, it's especially detrimental over the course of a very long race like the marathon. Also, Scott is a very heavy sweater, so the dehydration that bothers all marathoners can be insurmountable for him. And even though physically he can do very long runs, Scott gets bored once a run starts nearing 2 hours, so his psychological strengths aren't oriented toward the marathon. Relative to other runners, his talent lies in handling repeated loads of medium-paced runs of 60–80 minutes, so it's no surprise that his best races are in the middle range of road races.

As with me and my half mile time, you could argue that Scott's PRs are the way they are because of the type of training that he does, and that he could run equivalent times at other distances if he reoriented his training. There's some truth in that, but I think you're more likely to enjoy racing if you look at it from the other angle. That is, the type of training that you most prefer is likely the kind that you're best suited to physically and mentally, and training that way reinforces your talents at those distances you're best at. I keep coming back to the primacy of enjoying your running, and finding your best race distance is no exception. If you do the type of training that best suits you, you'll enjoy it more, and will be more likely to stick with it; from that will come better races.

One problem that runners who never ran in high school or college can have is experimenting with enough distances and types of training to find their best events. The 5K is the shortest distance that's commonly offered in road racing, and most people start running 10Ks, 10-milers and even marathons within their first year of running, because that's what's out there. Then they assume these longer races are their best distances, and structure their training toward those ends. This is different from how most elite runners find their best distance. As I said, I raced the half-mile in high school and college, and sometimes I even raced as short as the quarter-mile. I only moved up in distance as I aged and had tried my hand (and feet) at shorter races. Carlos Lopes, of Portugal, won the 1984 Olympic Marathon at age 37; he didn't run his first marathon until the previous year. In 1976, he had won the Olympic silver medal at 10,000 meters, and he started his career as a 1500 meter runner. And New Zealand's Rod Dixon won a bronze medal at 1,500 meters in 1972, took fourth at 5,000 meters in the 1976 Olympics, and won the New York City Marathon in 1983.

These runners certainly explored their talents at a variety of distances, and you should do the same. Don't say, "Oh, I'm not fast, so I must be a marathoner." Speed is relative. The only people we usually see running races of a mile and shorter are national- and world-class performers, whereas we're used to seeing everyone from speedy elites to people in their 80s running marathons. That doesn't necessarily mean that those 80-year-olds might not have better equivalent performances in the half mile. Search out competitive opportunities at as short a race as you can find, and give it a try a few times. You can also learn plenty from a good coach. He or she can watch how you run and what types of workouts you do best and can help you bypass some unnecessary pain. You would probably discover these things on your own, but it's nice not to have to go through that, because then you can enjoy your running more.

Finally, once you find your best distances, don't confine yourself to them. On the world-class level, we see runners race a few times at 3,000 meters, then produce a spectacular race at 5K or 10K. And from 3 to 6 months before the important part of their racing season starts, you're likely to see the same runners racing at longer than their target distances. For example, in 1995 Kenya's Ismael Kirui defended his title in the 5,000 meters at the World Championships. This race was in August. In March, he placed second at the World Cross Country Championships, which was a 12K race, and in April, he set a world record for 10 miles on the roads. In June and July, he ran several 3,000 meter races. The combination of strength from the longer races and the sharpness from the shorter races left him perfectly ready to tackle his specialty.

All racers can benefit from applying this approach. Every July, I run the Utica Boilermaker 15K, in Utica, New York, and the Quad-City Times Bix 7 Mile, in Davenport, Iowa. As part of my preparation for these races, I run two or three 5Ks in June. The 5K is far from my perfect race distance, but I know that a few good efforts in this short race will make the early pace of my longer, target races seem easier by comparison. Low-key, short races are also good to use as time trials or controlled, hard runs if you focus on longer races and have a hard time getting yourself to do speed work on a regular basis.

TRAINING TO RACE

I could let this section of the chapter fill this entire book, and some readers would still want more. Everyone wants to know how to make their running easier and how to improve; more specifically, racers want to know how they should structure their training to achieve their time or distance goals. Whether I speak at running clinics, or talk with fellow runners after a race, or run with a group at a running camp, the conversation eventually comes around to one topic: how can I run faster?

That's a good question. I can answer it for you in general terms, giving you some guidance about what elements should be part of your training program. But, unlike some, I'm not willing to lay down day-by-day schedules that I claim to be universally applicable to runners wanting to, for example, run a certain time for a 5K or the marathon. Lifetime running is essentially about self-discovery and continual experimenting. You need to find the types and frequency of workouts that work best for you and that you enjoy doing. I'm not going to say that to break 20:00 for 5K you should run x number of times per week, at this and that specific pace on this and that specific date. First, different runners take different routes to the same goal. Between, say, 1975 and 1977, Frank Shorter and I were pretty evenly matched in the marathon. I ran 2:09 to win the Boston Marathon in 1975; Frank ran 2:10 to win the silver medal in the 1976 Olympic Marathon. Yet we had vastly different training systems. Frank's was track-oriented; in addition to beating me at the 1976 Olympic Marathon Trials, he won the 10,000 meter final in the Olympic Trials, and at one point, he set the American record for the indoor 2-mile. I certainly did my speed work, and I even placed fourth in the '76 Trials 10,000, but my training for the marathon was based around building strength with consistent high mileage on the roads. Through plenty of experimenting and continual analysis of what worked for us as individuals, we had hit on different systems that got us to roughly the same place in the marathon.

I'm also hesitant to lay down set schedules because doing so can be an invitation to frustration. You've got to be flexible with your training. When training for the marathon was the focus of my life, I didn't have a day-by-day plan mapped out for the 3 months leading up to a big race. There's just too much that can happen—out of your control—that can influence your training, and you're just going to feel markedly different from run to run. This is even more so when you're trying to balance your training with demanding job and family responsibilities. I've noticed that, in the real world, if you lay down set schedules, something is going to intervene and throw you off that schedule. If your schedule says you must go to the track for speed work on Wednesday, and you get out of work late Wednesday, and it's pouring rain, are you really going to get in the best workout you're capable of? You're better off allowing yourself the flexibility to try the next day, when things might work out more in your favor. If it's Wednesday or nothing, it's likely to become nothing too often, and your training and racing will suffer.

Instead, I prefer to have my races planned well in advance, and work back from them in setting training goals. Say I have an important half marathon in 2 months. Then I know that I want to get in three or four long runs, three or four shorter races, two or three sessions of long repeats, such as mile intervals, and at least that many workouts of shorter repeats, such as half- or quarter-miles. Then I think of how to construct my time between now and the target race 2 months away so I'm able to do these key workouts at a good level of quality. I'll want to leave a few days between speed workouts, I'll want to alternate among speed workouts of various distances and I'll want to plan my long runs so they don't fall within 5 or so days before one of the shorter races. Even then, I have to be flexible. If I head out to run for 90 minutes or 2 hours, and it's 90 degrees and I'm struggling from step one, there's no law that says I have to run the allotted distance. As you run for a lifetime, you'll get better all the time about being able to sense when it's wise to back off, and when it's time to push. Your training will become more and more intuitive, and that will help to keep it fresh and exciting, rather than seeming as if it's carved in stone, and that you have to do what's been ordained regardless of what else is going on in your life.

Rae Baymiller: Late Start, Early Success

Rae Baymiller was running with her daughter Tanya in the 1992 Twin Cities Marathon when her child looked at her and said, "Mom, you go ahead." At first, motherly instinct vetoed the idea. "I didn't want to leave her," Rae recalls. "I didn't want to try and go it alone. At that point she was the mother and I was the child. I was afraid to try it by myself." Bolstered by her own offspring's encouragement, Rae moved ahead, turning to wave to Tanya as she went. Her running career hasn't looked back since.

Rae started running at age 49, when, 7 months before the event, she and Tanya formed a pact to run the Twin Cities race together. "Everyone kept telling me, 'You won't do it,'" she remembers. "Tanya was working and going to school in San Francisco and I was in New York. I guess my training was a little more comprehensive than hers, so I was able to run ahead." Despite her late start, Rae is now one of the premier age-group runners in the country. She holds American age-group records at 10 miles (1:02:01), the half marathon (1:19:40) and 25K (1:38:10), and she's run a 2:51 marathon.

Even with her almost-immediate success, however, she doesn't take her running for granted. "When I went to buy my first pair of shoes," she remembers "the lady told me running would change my life and I thought, 'Come on.' It turns out she was right." Although she has always led an active lifestyle, Rae has found her niche in running. "Girls weren't encouraged to take part in sports when I was in school. I played tennis, tried skiing, really, I did all kinds of sports, but

I was only mediocre at any of them. I crave participation in sports and being active. I need it like I need food."

Rae, a resident of New York City, also cites running as a source for her inner strength. Other obstacles aren't as formidable to her when she feels physically able. She's taken on different projects in her career as a freelance designer and illustrator, and she credits running with giving her more confidence. "I was running a race in Tokyo when I ripped my plantar fascia at four miles," she recalls. "I told myself I was going to finish the race and I did. After something like that, you feel like you can do almost anything."

Casting her inhibitions aside has worked well for Rae. At one track meet, she went to the starting line wearing a new pair of shoes. "They were too big for me," she laughs. "I was tripping just walking in them. A friend of mine said the only thing to do was to go out as hard as I could and get the race over with. I went out hard, hung on and won in a 1,500-meter race against people who have had more speed training."

Rae has set lofty goals for herself. She hopes to stay competitive with the younger folks in the 40–49 age group, as well as break 5 minutes for the mile. But you won't find her obsessing over times and performances. "I don't worry about what I've run. I worry about what I'm going to run. To be successful, you've got to keep moving."

Speed Work for All

To be honest, sometimes I don't like the term "speed work." It can throw people off, because when they think of speed, they think of sprinting. Many runners are too quick to doubt their abilities, so they think speed work isn't meant for people like them, because they can't run a great time for 100 meters. Well, don't worry—neither can I, and that's not what speed work is about, anyway.

If "speed work" intimidates you, think instead of "change of pace" training. Many runners do just steady pace running, in which they just run one pace all the time. This is especially true of beginners and runners who think they're never going to race, but also the case with many people who attend races week after week. That's too bad, because incorporating a variety of paces in your running is as much a part of a well-rounded program as is varying your distance, terrain, time of day that you run, who you run with, etc., not to mention supplementary activities such as stretching and strengthening exercises and other forms of aerobic work. What I'm saying is that all runners, no matter what their goals and whether they ever plan to race, will get more out of their running by making a conscious effort to run a variety of paces. You really only need to set aside a day a week for a true change of pace day; two at the most if you've run for a few years and are pointing toward an important race in the next 3 months or sooner.

If you don't do this type of training, you're limiting yourself and the enjoyment you can get from your running. Physiologically, speed work will develop more of your capabilities than nothing but steady running—your leg strength will be greater, your range of motion will be greater, your running form will be smoother, and your ability to take in and use oxygen will be improved. Obviously, for racers this translates into better performance, because you're doing training that's more specific to the demands of racing. But even nonracers will notice benefits, and not just because the variety in effort will keep your running more interesting. As your fitness increases by doing a weekly change of pace session, you'll find that your other runs become easier and, therefore, more enjoyable. You'll have more of a sense that you're making progress, and every day won't seem exactly like the one before and after it.

The track is the most common setting for speed work. It's a controlled environment—you can determine exactly how fast you're running for exactly what distance with exactly what amount of rest. It's a great place to get a reality check and to see where you are in your program. But I want to talk more about incorporating change of pace training into your regular road runs. It's not that I don't think you should do speed work on the track; some people love the objective feedback that only the track can deliver. Rather, my goal in this book is to encourage as many runners as possible to figure out how to make a well-rounded program that's logistically doable enough that they'll more readily keep at it for a lifetime. We all know anecdotally how speed, strength and range of motion can decline with age. Speed work is a great way to maintain your capabilities in these areas, so I think it's important to find a way to keep doing this type of running throughout all the years of your running career, and the more convenient it is to do that, the more likely it is you'll do it.

So let's consider speed work on the roads. That's where I do most of mine these days. The convenience aside, I think doing some of your speed training on the roads is a good idea for most runners, because it's likely most of your races will be on the roads. By mixing hard and easy running over your road courses, you're learning how to run fast and recover over a variety of terrains, as you do in a road race. For example, say you're doing a workout of six 2-minute repeats, with a 2-minute recovery jog after each hard segment, over a 7-mile road course. You'll likely find yourself starting repeats halfway up a hill, running some parts of others downhill, running one or two on the flat, and so on. This mimics your racing, and the more specifically you can do that, the more race ready you'll be.

If you've never incorporated change of pace running into your training, start with a small amount. After running easily for a mile or two, run at a relaxed hard pace for a minute. You should feel as if you could run this faster pace for 5 minutes or so; you don't want to run this all out. Run easy for a minute, giving your breathing a chance to return to normal, then repeat the faster segment. Start with five to seven of these pickups, and do this workout once a week for 3 weeks. After that, you can start adding to the length of your fast segments, or keeping them at a minute but doing more of them, or mixing fast segments of varying length. That's one of the interesting things about speed training, especially when you do it on the roads. You can do whatever you want to do, in whatever mixture appeals to you, and know that this one run each week is going to benefit you all the rest of the week.

Of course, if you want to reach your racing potential, you'll have to work harder, and you'll have to be more specific in targeting your speed work toward your desired race distance. In the training potpourri section, I've listed my approach to core speed workouts for 5K, 10K and the marathon. But don't be bound by these, and don't do the same workout week after week after week. You'll come to dread it, and there's greater physiological benefit to be had from varying the length of your repeats. Most top runners aim for 2 to 5 miles worth of hard running in a speed session, and they do a variety of types of intervals with a variety of rest intervals between. The longer repeats, such as mile intervals, teach you patience and prepare you for the feeling of a long race. The shorter repeats, such as quarter miles, really get you going, and they help make the pace of your races seem easier. If you haven't raced much and don't know your 5K and 10K race pace, then 5K race pace is usually 60–90 seconds faster per mile than your regular training pace.

There's more going on than that physiologically, of course, but you want to keep variety and freshness in your training. So the benefits that various types of speed work have for your running economy, lactate threshold, VO_2 max and other terms that exercise scientists like to use aside, let's not forget how much more interesting running will stay during your life by regularly sampling all of its permutations.

The Marathon

Now, from one end of the spectrum to the other. Almost all runners are fascinated by the marathon, and I can't blame them. After all, running it the best that I could was the focus of my life for nearly 20 years. Because of its combination of challenge, history and unpredictably, I think the marathon really is the ultimate endurance event, as much like a cliché as that might sound. Yes, there are longer races that require even more endurance, but the marathon has an element of speed in it for many runners; trying to hit on the right mix of the two is part of what's so intoxicating and, at times, confounding about the marathon.

So I never want to discourage people from setting high goals, but the marathon, more than any other event, requires caution and intelligence. It's not for everybody, at least right off the bat, and it's certainly not the place to try crash training. Sure, you can run it on very limited training. When I was in college, there was a fellow student who would run the Boston Marathon every year on less than a month of training. He would finish, but he'd be a cripple afterward. This was a college guy; think how much more of an injury risk his approach would be if he had been 20 years older. The marathon has such a strong pull on people—it's one of the hardest events in the world, but also achievable by almost anyone in the world. So I understand why some are irrational in their approach to it, but you want to run more than just that one race. That guy at Wesleyan never gave himself the chance, through a sane, drawn out buildup, to learn what running is really about. To him, it was all rush and pain. No wonder he stopped running every year after the marathon. You don't want to be like that. You want to run for years and years, not just one race. There's always going to be some risk associated with training for the marathon, but you want to minimize it; a major way to do that is to set the marathon aside until you've been running regularly for at least a year. Also, don't think about building up to one if you're struggling with an injury. That injury is only going to get worse as you up your mileage. When you start to build toward a marathon that's 3 to 6 months away, you want to be able to honestly say to yourself, "I'm ready to handle the work."

The key to that work is the long run. One of the hardest aspects of training for the marathon is the timing of your long runs. You should build your long runs by a mile or two a week until you've reached 20 miles; then, ideally, you should do three or four 20-milers and one 22–24-miler. And your last long run should be no more than 2 weeks before your marathon, 3 if you're going to try the 22–24-miler. So you can see that by planning to do three long runs a month, you're talking about starting your buildup long before your marathon. The fall is considered marathon season, but think what this means for your long runs—you're going to be doing many of them in the summer, which is the worst time of the year for this type of running. I'm not saying it can't or shouldn't be done—I won the New York City Marathon, when it was held in October, 4 times—just that you need to be that much more careful with your long runs if you're doing them during the summer.

I see so many inexperienced runners out training in the hottest part of the day. That's going to make you tired, not tough. The training is tough enough on its own. Learn to think like experienced runners do—always be thinking, "How can I structure my training so I can recover from it the most quickly? What can I do in my life that will make that next workout easier?" This doesn't mean you should obsess over every detail of your life, but pay some attention to the little things. Beginners don't have the same sense as experienced runners of how what they're doing right now might affect them on their next run. This pertains to eating, drinking, commuting, how you sit, etc. Everything affects how you feel when you run, and this is especially the case when you're training in the summer for a fall marathon. That's part of why I always did so well at the Boston Marathon—it's ideally situated in terms of timing. I could train through the winter, and the long runs and mileage would make me stronger, not break me down, as they often do in the summer. Many people think the summer is the key time of the year for running. They don't know that the winter can be the best time to train for a marathon, so long as your footing isn't inhibited. Don't rule out spring marathons. You'll probably find that your long runs for them are easier than when you have to do them in the summer for fall events.

I almost never went farther than 20 miles in my long runs, but I used to run three to four marathons a year, so that gave me a good background. If you're doing just one marathon a year, then going beyond 20 miles once or twice in the 3 to 6 weeks before your race can give you a lot of confidence. Be careful, though, and only do it if it makes sense. It's hard for me to say what each individual should do; much of it has to do with what you're doing elsewhere in your life. If your job is demanding, and your weekends are busy running errands, and you find the 20-milers to be challenge enough, then you're probably better off leaving your long runs at that. In addition to the greater injury risk that can come from doing too long of a long run, you're also risking almost exponentially greater fatigue. In 1990, I did a 25-miler 3 weeks before Boston after having raced the day before. I was with a group on a long run, and I wasn't feeling all that great, but I was pushing for the marathon, and I was giving my training everything extra that I had. I was 42, though, and didn't know yet how to adjust my training to allow for more recovery as I aged. I got through the 25-miler OK, but I never felt comfortable in the race, and I ran 2:20 to take fifth in the masters race. I was in better shape than that; because of the lingering fatigue it caused, the 25-miler just 3 weeks before detracted from my marathon.

This is an example of the types of adjustments that veteran marathoners have to make as they age. Unfortunately, many runners take the opposite approach once they become a master. It's pretty common when you enter a new age group to get so psyched that you overdo it and forget some of the basics. Suddenly, you're training harder than you have for 5 years, and although that drive is admirable, it doesn't take into account that those 5 extra years mean you need to be that much more careful about adequate rest. I'm not saying you can't train hard—you can reach phenomenal levels—just that it gets trickier. Also, beware of the outside stresses in your life. You're likely to have a busier life at age 40 than you did at 30—family, more responsibility at work, etc. You always have to give these factors their proper respect, or they'll inhibit your training.

Although I've retired from racing marathons for now, there is a certain attraction in starting again after I turn 50 in December 1997. It would be nice to come out of marathon retirement, break the American age group record, then put the event away again. If I do this, I'll do more systematic crosstraining than I do now, and certainly more than I did in the '70s and '80s. I'll concentrate more on weights and stretching, and I'll regularly supplement my running with swimming, rowing and cycling. That's because I would want as good an aerobic base as possible, but I know that if I tried to train like I used to, I wouldn't make it to the starting line because of injury. Another thing that 50+ marathoners should take special care with is strengthening their back. Most marathoners of that age will have had sedentary jobs for more than 20 years, and all that time being deskbound has taken its toll on your back's strength and flexibility. A strong back will help you maintain form better on the long runs you'll be doing before the marathon, so regular stretching and strengthening of the back should be part of all 50+ marathoners' programs.

Regardless of age, all marathoners should use shorter races as part of their buildup. You don't have to run these all out; use them as hard training efforts twice a month, one at a shorter distance (5K to 10K), the other longer (15K to half marathon). There are many people training for marathons who have never raced, and going to shorter races is especially helpful for them. In addition to the training benefits of the effort, these give you a chance at dress rehearsal and to learn what your race-day routine should be. Try to simulate how you anticipate the marathon will be, and learn from your mistakes. On marathon day, you'll be better prepared for little matters, such as how much time to allot for the Porta Potties, dealing with pre-race nervousness and learning how to run in a large crowd, that can have a profound impact on your marathon and can really throw you for a loop if you haven't experienced them before.

TRAINING AND RACING POTPOURRI

I attend more than 25 races a year, and I talk with thousands of runners every year. Here are my thoughts on some of the most common training and racing questions that I'm asked, as well as a few observations about mistakes I regularly see other runners make.

How Fast on Long Runs?

Many runners are confused about how fast they should do their long runs. Some, it seems, want to believe that there's a single way to train that's universally applicable, such as, "Do your long runs 13.8 percent slower per mile than your 12K

ONE RUNNER'S SUCCESS WITH WEIGHT TRAINING

Weight training has gotten an undeserved bad rap among distance runners. The thinking is, why would you want to spend all that time running to get slim and speedy, only to bulk up with a lot of big muscles that will slow you down? For many runners, weight lifting conjures images of macho types in sweaty gyms or fitness faddists trying out the latest in Home Shopping gadgetry. That's too bad, because weight training, by helping you to stay strong, can help you to keep running, which is the main goal. I'll offer Gail's case as an example.

For years, she had the good fortune of running virtually injury-free. The injuries she did get were minor, and she was able to recover from them and return to her desired level of running quickly. In those years, she had tried lifting weights a few times, but she had always lost interest; she figured that if she worked her heart muscle hard enough, then the rest of them could fend for themselves. This changed during her second pregnancy, when her back let her know that she had neglected it for 39 years. She kept thinking the pain she was feeling there would right itself, but every night she would sleep fitfully, then drag herself through the next day hoping that her back would loosen up.

She finally sought help from a physical therapist, who figured out that the baby had pushed Gail's rib cage so far back her ribs had almost become detached from her vertebrae. Obviously, running for all those years had done nothing for her back muscles. The physical therapist assured her that weight training would.

Reluctantly, Gail began some light weight training in our dark, musty basement. To her surprise, the pains went away, and she could sleep through the night! Figuring that she was cured, she quit for awhile, and the pain came back. Gail realized that she would have to commit to this for a long time. She also knew that she had to get out of that basement, so she joined a nearby gym to have access to a variety of equipment and some instruction. Her back was getting better, but the whole regimen was taking too much time. How was she going to find time to run and do the weight lifting that she had become convinced she needed?

A friend who is a fitness director at a local YMCA helped. He showed Gail how doing several sets of many repetitions of light weights doesn't really build strength and takes too much time. (She already knew the latter.) Lots of women and distance runners do this low-weight, high-rep approach because they're afraid of getting bulky or of being slowed down by big muscles. Gail's friend explained that only certain people—those with the right genes who spend hours a day lifting massive weights—are going to get that bodybuilder look, just as only certain people with the right genes who train all the time are going to look and run like me. The rest will gain strength, but not unwanted bulk.

On any given exercise, Gail's friend had her lift the weight between 8 and 12 times. The trick was to "fail," or be unable to do another repetition with proper form, on the 12th repeat. If, on the 12th repeat, she could still lift the weight and maintain good form, then it was time to increase the amount of weight she was using for that exercise. If not, she'd work on that amount of weight until she surpassed 12 repetitions. Not only does this build strength, but it does so quickly and efficiently.

In our 40s, it's a great feeling to notice real physical improvement in strength, posture and so on. Gail preaches this gospel to all who will listen, especially women, who might not have grown up developing muscular strength, as many men have. Studies have shown weight training to be very effective in preventing osteoporosis in older women. For younger women, it pays to develop strong muscles and bones early on to help offset the difficulties that women experience in their post-menopausal years.

Look at an older person walking down the street. If you don't see the wrinkled face and gray hair, what tells you about that person's age? The short steps, the stiff gait, the bent posture. The stronger you go into that phase of life, the better off you'll be. Many runners probably think running makes them strong enough, but go to the finish of a road race, and you'll see otherwise. An elite runner who is struggling at the end of a race is still able to hold himself upright no matter how tired he is. Then watch the slower runners and find the ones having a tough day. They almost always bend at the middle and lose their form completely. The top runners' superior strength is partly genetic, but partly acquired, and less gifted runners can obtain that same kind of strength to help maintain good form. This will mean fewer injuries.

Some of the best runners I've known, such as former American record holders in the marathon Alberto Salazar and Patti Lyons Catalano (now Dillon), used to spend hours weight training; they didn't have an ounce of bulk on their frames. If you see a runner who looks bulky from weights, it usually means that person has been lifting a lot of donuts as well (present company included). And weight training won't stiffen you up, either. As your muscles and connective tissues become stronger, they'll also become more supple, and your flexibility will probably increase.

race pace, unless there's a full moon and the stock market is down." In the real world, pacing on your long runs depends on a number of factors: the weather, your racing schedule and which distance you prefer to race. Do you race 15K or more at least once a month? If you do, you should do your 15–20 mile training runs at an easy pace that you know you can maintain to the finish. Your long runs count as hard days just because of the distance that you're covering, so your normal training pace is fine most of the time. It's especially important to start at a moderate pace when it's hot and/or humid; there are few things more discouraging in your training than struggling the last part of a long run because you were overly ambitious at the start. When training for the marathon, I used to begin my long runs slowly, but if I felt OK, I'd push the pace when I approached the middle or two-thirds mark. When in doubt, ease up a bit and don't push the pace until you sense you won't have to slow down before the end of the run. Skip your long run if you raced hard for 15K or more the day before.

How Easy Before Speed Work?

Another big source of confusion is how easy to take it in the day or two before a speed workout. Some people think it's a good idea not to lower their mileage or intensity before such a workout, because they think that going into the workout tired and then trying to run hard will better simulate the conditions they'll face in a race. This is a mistake; it's wise to rest before your speed workouts. Let your body and mind recover from your recent training so you'll be able to put forth a solid effort on your hard training days. Overall, you'll get fitter as a result of running faster on your hard days and a bit slower on other days than you will by having to compromise the quality of your speed work because of a faster pace on your recovery days. Masters runners, especially, should plan well-deserved easy days before and after speed work, because with age we need more time to recover from hard efforts. We can often maintain a high level of quality in our hard efforts as we get older if we remember to do them a bit less frequently.

Even if you run easy in the day or two before a speed workout, many times you'll still feel tired on the day of the workout. Perhaps you've been training hard the past few weeks, it has been hot and humid, or you've had a tiring few days at work. Even under such circumstances, when I begin my speed workouts, I usually discover that my fatigue fades away (although as a 48-year-old, I seem to be tired all the time!). We often "get tired" when there's a hard effort ahead of us. I defuse apprehension about a hard speed workout by carefully warming up, drinking lots of water before, thinking of my upcoming races against certain runners and telling myself I'll just do the best I can on that day.

How Often to Do Speed Work?

Many runners, especially those who come to running late in life, have little confidence in their speed. If you started running as an adult, then it's likely that you've had little or no exposure to regular track training and racing, as likely would a younger runner or an adult runner who has been at it since high school. These "speedless" runners sometimes make one of two mistakes—they either never run fast in training, thus making their lack of confidence self-fulfilling, or they try to overcompensate by doing speed work all year long. I've mentioned elsewhere why incorporating various paces in your running is important for anyone who wants to race, so here I'll address the overzealous runners who run fast throughout the year.

To get the most out of your running over a lifetime, it's important not to do hard speed training 12 months a year. I've come close to doing so on numerous occasions, but it becomes tedious, fatiguing and injury-inducing. After a few months, continuous racing and/or speed work will actually make you lose conditioning and go beyond your peak level of fitness. Instead, you should pick out the events that are important to you and train for them over a 3-month cycle. This will give you time to recover physically and mentally. Don't do any speed work for 4 to 6 weeks after a peak period and at the beginning of your buildup. Instead, develop your speed by doing other types of training, such as hill repeats, bounding, weight work and striders, that keep your fast-twitch muscle fibers activated but don't stress your body the way that going to the track once or twice a week do. After 4 to 6 weeks of that, you'll be ready to focus on developing your speed the more traditional way by doing intervals.

How Does Bill Do Speed Work?

I now do my speed work on the roads rather than on the track. The roads are more convenient; there's not as much pressure to hit specific times; and there's not as much risk of injury as there is when going around the curves on the track. I wear racing shoes for my workouts; a person's biomechanics when doing speed work are slightly different, so it makes sense to wear shoes designed for faster running.

Before a speed workout, I do a 2-mile warm-up; if I'm training for a longer race, I'll do a longer one. I cool down with a mile or so of easy running. Also, before and after each workout, I do three or four 100-meter pickups. In all my workouts, I run faster than race pace for the distance I'm training for, and I keep the rest short. Here are some examples of workouts that I try to do when aiming for various popular distances:

5K

Distance: 12–16x400 meters
Recovery: 30–60 seconds after each
Pace: about 10 seconds per mile faster than 5K race pace

10K

Distance: 6–8x1,000 meters
Recovery: 60 seconds after each
Pace: a few seconds per mile faster than 5K race pace

Marathon

Distance: 4–6x1,500 meters/mile
Recovery: 60 seconds after each
Pace: between 5K and 10K race pace

Speed Work During Times of Stress?

At the other extreme, many busy runners are quick to abandon high-quality work when their personal lives become too stressful. As I mentioned above, it's normal to feel more tired than usual on the days when you know that a hard workout awaits you after a hard day at the office. It's usually best to at least start these workouts and frequently discover that you're not as tired as you thought.

Steve Stovall: Racing Through Life

There are many runners who are faster than Steve Stovall. There are many runners who run more than Steve Stovall. But you'd be hard-pressed to find many runners who embody the positive spirit of competition more than Steve Stovall.

Steve, a resident of Princeton, New Jersey, ran his first race, a 2-miler, in 1976 at age 35. He had started running 5 years earlier to lose weight and to earn points in Ken Cooper, M.D.'s aerobic points system, beginning with a mile a day and building to regular 3-milers. So, after debuting with a 2-miler in October 1976 and having such a reasonable progression, what was Steve's next race? "In January '77," he recalls, "I ran the Jersey Shore Marathon. I ran 3:11 in a blizzard. I was crying when I finished, and not because I was happy." As did many runners of his generation, Steve thought that being a runner in the late 1970s and early 1980s meant one thing only—being a marathoner. Then, he saw the light. "My marathoning lasted until 1984," he says. "I ran thirteen of them. I stopped because I hate the marathon—the preparation, the last part, and I hate how depleted I get and how long it takes me to recover."

That last point is key for Steve, because even though his 2:45 PR (personal record) at age 40 showed some talent at the marathon, he thought that it wasted his time, namely, his racing time. "I diddled around with biathlons and triathlons from age fifty-one until 1995," he says. "Then, I wanted to get back to running. Racing the 5K is my obsession. I can run a lot of them and see how I'm doing from week to week. [He raced 15 times in 1995.] After all this time, even though I know I'm not going to PR anymore, competition is still my primary motivation. [Steve placed in the top three in his age group in all but one of his 1995 races.] There's certainly no other reason for me to get up at 5:40 every morning to train, other than that other guy in his fifties who is rolling over and going back to sleep."

Steve rightfully says that his biggest challenge is the constraints on his time. He's employed as a project manager for a book developer, he's a volunteer firefighter, he's a part-time teacher of advertising at Rider University and he's the father of four children. Every workday, he rises at 5:40, rides an exercise bike for half an hour, runs for just under 40 minutes, rides another 15 minutes, crams in a few minutes of sit-ups and stretching, and only then gets ready for work. Twice a week, including once on the weekend, he does the track workouts that are necessary for success in his target distance. "By now this is second nature to me," Steve claims. "If I had to think in the morning, I would be in big trouble."

Of course, Steve recognizes other benefits from his running besides the thrill of competition. "I'm sure my family would tell you that it makes me a better person to be around," he says, "and I know that it gives me peace of mind. With my personality, I might be an alcoholic or a workaholic if I couldn't channel a lot of myself into running."

What about the future, when Steve acknowledges that he'll have to deal with the process of slowing down? "Yes, I won't be able to train as vigorously," he concedes. "But even when I'm eighty, I want to be one of the top three eighty-year-olds at the local races."

Other times, though, your fatigue is more well-founded, such as when you've been putting in extra hours at the office for an extended period. In those circumstances, it's usually best to skip regular track workouts, because you'll probably not run up to your capabilities, and you'll likely feel more frustrated afterward. Instead, do an unstructured fartlek (Swedish term for "speed play") run once a week. The reason is that "speed play" leaves you free to go as hard or easy as you feel. To prepare for hill repeats or intervals on a track seems to demand too much physical and psychological attention when you're really struggling in another part of your life. After warming up for at least 10 minutes, try to include 10–15 minutes' worth of hard running, in 30-second to 3-minute bursts, within one of your regular road courses. With these, you'll be able to maintain nearly all of your anaerobic fitness until your crisis period passes.

When doing the fartlek, ease into the hard work; you may surprise yourself with how hard you may go over various distances. I also caution you about doing these sessions with a friend. I've done this and found myself feeling like we were overdoing it—almost testing each other, as if we were in a race and we were side by side. This is quite different from running quarters or 800s, drafting behind each other on the track secure in the knowledge that "today we're running 10 or 12 or 14 efforts with a specific rest period." If you do run fartleks with a friend, set some guidelines for your hard efforts, or you may find yourself in a duel, exacerbating your situation rather than helping it.

Should All Racers Warm Up?

I'm always surprised when, at a road race, even in the half hour before the start, I see many runners who aren't warming up. This leaves them susceptible to two of the most common mistakes that runners of all ages make. They're unprepared to go out at their proper pace, and either start too fast and slow down too much by the end, or they spend the first part of the race getting going and have too much left over at the end. A longer or more intense warm-up might help them to adjust more easily to the harder pace in the first mile. I find I need half an hour of easy running, stretching and four to six 100–150 meter pickups to get ready for the early part of a race. We know that it's an advantage to go to the start with your heart rate elevated; keep it elevated by jogging in place those final minutes before the start. Also, be sure to start with folks who are going at about your race pace, and don't be overly concerned about blasting away from the line. Often the best result comes from an easy start, a gradual increase in pace and a strong finish. Remember, this was the race strategy of the great Lasse Viren, who won the 5K and 10K in both the 1972 and 1976 Olympics.

Are Layoffs a Good Idea?

Some runners are skeptical when they hear that some of the best runners in the world take breaks of a week or longer in which they do no running. These breaks make a good deal of physiological and psychological sense; running is how these people make their livings, and they've worked so hard before a peak effort that they look forward to a break just like you might look forward to a week of vacation, regardless of how much you like your job.

I have a week or two each year when I don't run, or do very little running. I do this in December when the road race season is pretty much over. When I used to train for the marathon in my 20s and 30s, I didn't do this; I was always training for a marathon! I'd often fail miserably in at least one of these races, and even my "youthful energy" couldn't keep me from catching the flu, becoming overly fatigued, etc. during this period.

Unlike track, our sport can be competed in year round, but such attempts sooner or later lead to injury or sickness. I really look forward to my break at the end of November. During most of the year, I run twice a day, 3 to 4 days a week. I'm not sure that it's necessary to train twice on each of those 3 or 4 days, but I can tell you, I enjoy the one-a-day short jogs and complete rest days with no running even more.

I have discovered in recent years that I seem to plateau, or even slow down, in June, July and August races, and I know it's not just the heat. Usually, I've run 10 to 12 races from February to the end of May. I've reached a peak of sharpness and strength, and now my body and mind want a rest.

RACING STRATEGIES

Racing is all about rationing your resources. You can do the greatest training in the world, and blow it all by running stupidly. I should know, because at times I've thought that I've done the greatest training in the world, and I've blown it by racing stupidly. In 1982, I ran the Rio de Janeiro Marathon. In the first 8 miles, a runner who I didn't know was forcing the pace. I thought that as the defending champion I should keep him within striking distance, even though I knew going with him at the fast pace he was running wasn't the best thing for my race. This cost me big time. He dropped out a few miles later; I don't know if he was a rabbit or just someone who didn't know what he was doing, but I took him to be a serious contender, and let him alter my race plan. The day turned out to be hotter than I thought, and the weather, combined with my eager early pace, really drained me, and I dropped out before reaching 20 miles. If I had used a moderate start, taken the heat into account more and run *my* race, not that of someone who I had never even seen before, I would have done much better, and probably would have been able to repeat as the winner. Sometimes you have to let your emotions take over, and race aggressively even if the rational part of your brain is telling you otherwise, but the first half of a hot weather marathon is hardly the place!

In my more sane moments, I use the same basic race strategy regardless of the distance. I employ a slow start, a hard push in the middle and then I try to hang on until the finish. This is what suits my body and temperament best, and my training is designed to help me race this way. More runners could benefit from using this approach. A large percentage of racers, especially inexperienced ones, are overly anxious at the start and take off way too hard for the first mile. Inevitably, they slow, and find themselves struggling mentally as the race progresses. Using my strategy, I go out at a reasonable pace—it's fast enough that I can keep my opponents in sight, but it's gentle enough so that my body doesn't go into shock at what I'm suddenly asking it to do. As I feel more fluid and warmed up, I notch the pace to another level, and start picking off runners who misjudged their early pace. If you've ever passed people in the last two-thirds of a race, you know what a great psychological boost this is. Yes, you may be just as tired as the runner you're catching, but he or she doesn't have to know that! The runners you pass aren't likely to be able to stay with you for more than a hundred yards. Then you can move on the next target. By the time you're near the finish, you're probably as ready as those around you to kick to the finish.

I model my training toward this end. In my prime, if I was doing eight half-mile repeats, I'd do the first one in 2:15. I'd work the next few down to 2:12–2:13, and then on the fifth one try to throw in a 2:08. On the last few, I'd return to running 2:12s. This complemented my relative strengths against my opponents—when I would surge against better kickers in the second half of a race, I would think that doing so was no different than what I had done in training. I knew that I could make that one big push and get away, and then return to what was still a hard pace and keep running consistently while tired from the surge. Others whose biggest weapon against their opponents was mid-race strength, such as Steve Prefontaine and Brendan Foster, also structured their training the same way. I'll do the same on my long runs—I start at an easy pace, and once I feel like all the cylinders are firing, I push it a bit over the last half of the run. To be able to surge is the key when you're battling with a specific opponent. This is true for all levels of runners, but to achieve this, you have to train for it.

I'm not suggesting that this is how you must race; rather, that you should go into each race with some idea of how you want to attack the course and distance on that day given your level of fitness, the weather, and so on. Sometimes I realize just before or during a race that on that day, I'm going to have to adjust my basic strategy. For example, if the first half mile of the race is a straight shot down the road, then I can use my usual slow start and take a couple of minutes to build into a faster pace. But if there's a sharp turn just 200 yards after the start, then I'm going to have to approach it differently. People are going to be scrambling to make that first turn unfettered, so they're likely to go out even faster than they usually do. That's never been my style, and now that I'm older, I'm that much more limited in how fast I can run the first few hundred yards without really paying for it later. So I'll line up on the opposite side of the road that the turn is on—if it's a right hand turn, I line up on the left side of the field—so I can take the corner wide. As another example, if I know that there's a big uphill in the last half mile of a race, then I won't push as hard in the middle as I otherwise would, so I'll have a little something extra for the end.

You'll notice that these examples assume some knowledge

of the course. The more you know about what the terrain will be like throughout the race, the more intelligently you can run. During your pre-race warmup, check out the start and finish areas. Note when the first turn is, whether the road suddenly narrows soon after the start, whether the finish line is just 200 yards past the final turn, and so on. If you know these little things about the course, you can talk yourself through the course better. For example, say you ran past the finish area during your warmup, and you noticed that after a long, straight stretch, the course turns and finishes 100 yards later. The runners who don't know the course will be despairing during that straight stretch and wondering if and when the race is ever going to end. You, in contrast, will be able to orient yourself on the course, ration your physical and psychological resources appropriately, and make that final turn with just enough left for a strong last 100 yards. Your opponents are likely to be surprised by its abruptness, and won't be able to shift gears in time to take advantage of the final stretch. Always warm up over as much of the course as possible, especially the first and last half miles. If you can't investigate both, check out the finish. By that point, you're going to need all the help you can get, and knowing what's in store over the final few minutes of a race is a tremendous help.

Many runners, of course, are battling the clock more than specific opponents. Research has consistently shown that the best results come from an even pace. Look at the world records run on the track. In the distance events these days, these are usually achieved by a runner who is paced for the first half of the race, then left on his or her own for the second half. The record setter is usually so far ahead of everyone else that he or she is running only against time. In most of these cases, the splits are amazingly even from lap to lap. For example, in June 1995, Ethiopia's Haile Gebre Silasie ran a world record of 26:43.53 for 10,000 meters. (This is averaging 4:18 per mile for 6.2 miles!) His first 5,000 meters took

13:21.71; his second, 13:21.82. You can't run a more even pace than that.

The same approach works whether you're trying to break 27:00 or 47:00 for 10K. Experienced runners have a good grasp of what they're capable of handling on a given day, and they pace themselves accordingly. They know it's easy to feel surprisingly good for the first third of a race, but that giving in to the delusion that a fast start will help them build a bulge for when they slow later usually becomes self-defeating. That is, go out too fast, and you'll definitely slow, and you'll wind up running slower than you're capable of on that day. You want always to be running within yourself physically and mentally. The more you've simulated this in your training, the better you'll be able to do this. To me, this is one of the main benefits of doing regular speed work. The physical benefits aside, you gain a valuable sense of what you can handle, and you can dole out your efforts in a race more intelligently. Also, you can be more confident and not worry as much about how others around you are running. You can't let others' performances affect you; you have to race according to how you've prepared. When you figure that out, you'll run your best races.

Doug Mock: Focus on Fleetness

Doug Mock, of Germantown, Maryland, is like many runners. He simply wants to see how fast he can run. With PRs of 14:15 for 5K and 29:57 for 10K, however, he's unlike most runners in that he's able run fast at almost a national-class level. But don't let those fast times fool you into thinking the only thing to be learned from Doug is how quickly to do your half-mile repeats.

"My outlook is that I never want to look back and wonder how fast I could have been," Doug says. At age 29, with just more than 10 years of base and progression behind him,

Doug is in what should be his peak years for distance racing. He's also blessed with a fair amount of natural speed—he's run 3:52 for 1,500 meters, or roughly a 4:10 mile—and the ability to focus on long-term goals. "To me, running is a sport. I view running as training for racing." Now be honest—if you were in Doug's speedy shoes, would you do any differently?

The thing is, even though you probably will never run as fast as Doug, you don't have to do things differently than him. "People know that I'm a runner," Doug says, "and I get asked a lot about how my racing is going. I like that—it's a major part of my identity. I'm a pretty quiet guy. I love going somewhere where somebody is mouthing off about how much money he makes or how important he is, and I don't say anything, but inside I'm thinking, 'The only thing that's in shape on him is his mouth.' You don't have to have broken thirty minutes in the 10K to give you that kind of confidence."

Doug, who says "I enjoy being healthy and in shape," helps others do so as a fitness instructor at a health club. Seeing others pursue other activities further focuses his attention on getting the most out of his running. "I see people in shape from doing other things," he says, "and I'm like a little kid outside the window looking in. Running has made me realize that I always want to be active, but it won't always have to be devoted to running. Once I realize that I've stopped improving, I'll keep running, but won't race, and I'll focus on other things."

"Well," he adds with a laugh, "that's easy to say now. We'll see what happens when I turn forty."

THE PSYCHOLOGICAL SIDE

When you're testing the limits of your potential, racing can be harder mentally than physically. After all, your body is in pretty substantial distress, and your mind's main task seems to be to figure out how to better the situation as soon as possible. If they could be illustrated, the battles that go on in racers' minds would be far more interesting to watch unfold than would be most road races. That's one of the things I love most about running—thanks to what it takes to push yourself, you really get to know yourself, and what kind of mental toughness you have. Once you've realized what you're capable of, and that the negative voice inside your head shouldn't always win, this can have a powerful impact on how you conduct the rest of your life.

But back to the mind during racing itself. You should try to talk to yourself constantly in a race. Assess how you're doing, how you might be able to notch it up a bit, and continually tell yourself how well you're doing, what you've already accomplished, and what you have left to do. During my races, I talk myself through the whole thing. "OK," I'll tell myself, "you're putting out a pretty darned good effort. Now, can you go a little harder at this stage of the race? Can you catch that guy 30 feet ahead of you? He's probably a lot more tired than you are." I don't think I'm a particularly tough runner mentally, but I've learned the tricks of the trade. You can beat people who might be as fit as you by talking yourself through a race with positive remarks. In longer races, I often keep telling myself, "Stay steady, stay steady." This helps me to keep doling out a pretty hard effort throughout the race, so I know when I get to the finish I've done about the best I could on that day, and if someone beats me, so be it. The more you compete, the better you are at assessing how much of your potential you've reached on a given day.

No matter what distance I'm racing at, I tell myself how much farther I have to go, especially in the latter stages. You want to do this from a positive standpoint—tell yourself, "OK, only 10 minutes to go. Think about how many times you've run for 10 minutes." It can help to focus on your training in these instances. You could say, "I know where 10 minutes of running from my house is. I've done that so many times. That's all I have to do now." With a mile to go at the Boston Marathon, I used to tell myself, "I ran 5:00 for the mile when I was a sophomore in high school. That's all I have to do now—run one 5:00 mile. I did that when I was 15, so I can do it now." Or in a 5K I'll think about my speed work, and tell myself how much training I've done at race pace. I'll say, "All I have to do in this last half mile of the race is run one pickup like I do in training. I've done that so many times. I know what the pace feels like. I know it's not going to kill me. Surely I can run this pace for just another couple of minutes."

Unfortunately, a lot of runners' self-talk during races is negative. They'll run the first mile too fast and get in distress too early in the race, and then notice that they're slowing down every mile. The more they remind themselves of this, the more tired they get, and the slower they run. It's a vicious cycle. In those circumstances, the best you can do is attempt to recover, finish strongly, and look at the race as a learning experience. Maybe you need to do more speed work at race pace so you'll have a better sense of what you can realistically handle.

But there are going to be races in which you feel sub-par, or your splits are going to be off, regardless of how intelligently you start. There are a few factors to consider here. First, if your time seems slow but you feel as if you're running decently, switch to a second goal—do the best you can on that day in relationship to the other runners in the race. If you ran strongly, but your time is off what you had expected, it's likely that most others' were, too, probably because of the weather or terrain. Second, your performances are going to have a certain ebb and flow to them. You have to accept that you aren't going to be constantly improving in every race.

The top runners in the world race frequently throughout the year, but they have a 2- to 3-month period in which they try to peak. They view their races during the other parts of the year as stepping stones to the most important events of the year. Finally, there's always a reason for how you're feeling. If you feel horrible during a race, and your time is substantially slower than your training indicates it should be, it may be a sign you're coming down with a cold or virus, or that your performances have plateaued and started to decline. In either case, it's time to step back, check your training log for clues and low key it for awhile.

Staying Healthy

INJURY TREATMENT AND AVOIDANCE

Structure your running so that you can avoid injury and keep doing it. Stretching and strengthening are like wearing good running shoes, eating healthfully and so on—if you get in the habit of doing them, your running will be easier and, therefore, better.

If you run everyday until you're 90 years old, I guarantee that you'll live a long life. I know that's simplistic, and a bit flippant, but there's an important kernel of truth in that statement. The key to running for a lifetime is really quite simple—keep running throughout your life. Ask any long-time runner what's the secret to his or her longevity, and you'll find out it's not diet or stretching or any other facet of fitness that some people obsess over. It's consistency. Ultimately, my goal is to be consistent.

The best way to be able to do that is to keep your body healthy. In high school, I once suffered from shin splints, and I had a brief flare-up during my 4 years at Wesleyan University. After college, from 1973 to 1992, I averaged more than 100 miles a week, I raced 25 times a year and I never missed more than 3 consecutive days of running, with one exception, when I had plantar fasciitis. Yes, I'm an efficient runner, I'm light and I was blessed with strong connective tissue. Still, the reason I've been able to pursue my running to the level I want for so long is because I haven't had major injuries. That's no fluke. I've always known that the main goal is to structure your running so you can keep doing it, and I've acted accordingly. In this chapter, I'll cover some of the major running injuries as well as look at elements of your training that can go a long way toward helping you avoid them.

INJURIES

Almost every time a journalist talks to me, there's a pointed question about injuries. It's clear to me, after years of hearing this question (from the nonrunning public, it's the first ques-

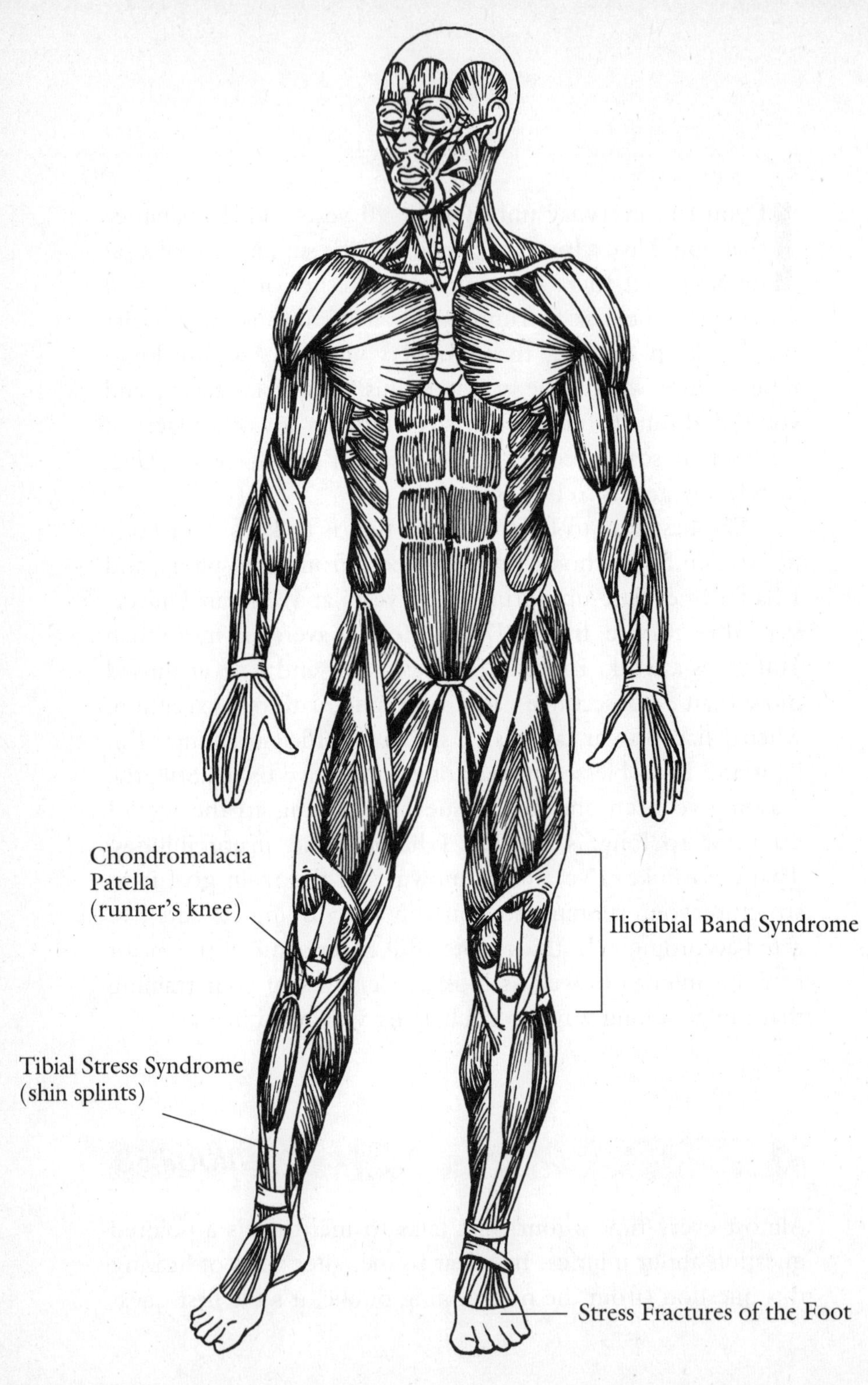
Chondromalacia
Patella
(runner's knee)
Iliotibial Band Syndrome
Tibial Stress Syndrome
(shin splints)
Stress Fractures of the Foot

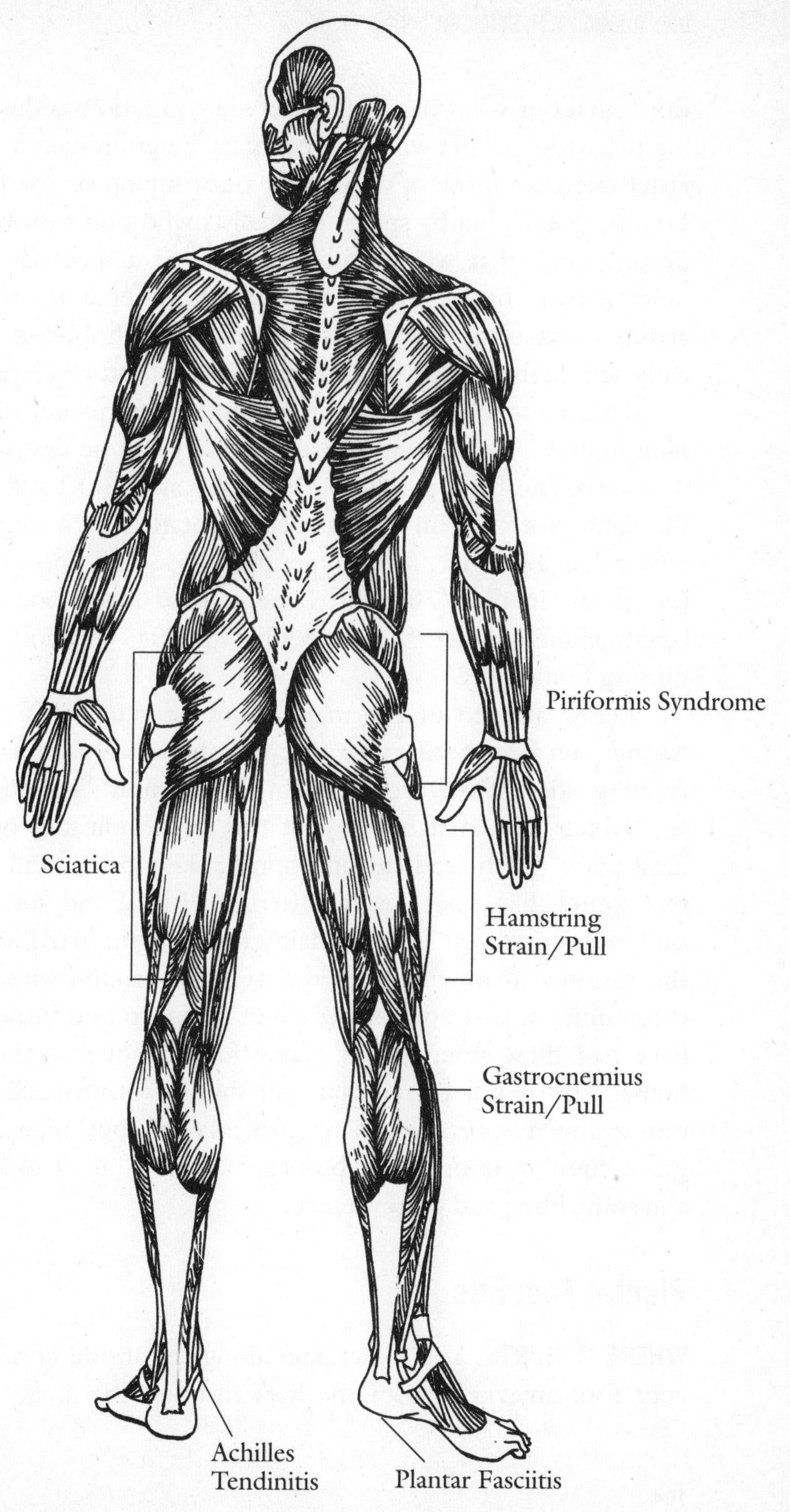
Piriformis Syndrome
Sciatica
Hamstring
Strain/Pull
Gastrocnemius
Strain/Pull
Achilles
Tendinitis
Plantar Fasciitis

tion), that our sport has an undeserved reputation as the great injurer. Most people who are sedentary deteriorate at a much faster rate than those of us who are out running on the roads. Yet, the public, led by sports journalists who don't probe too deeply, think that we're leading people to a sport that will destroy their backs, buckle their joints, cripple them with arthritis and ruin their knees, leaving them hobbling at an early age. Perhaps they've confused us with football players.

That's not to belittle the significance or frequency of running injuries. They are very real, and they can be devastating to your physical and psychological well-being. But I still think that our sport has an undeserved reputation as a negative, rather than a positive, force in people's lives. All I know is that the people in their 70s who I see at road races look much healthier and happier than the people in their 70s who I see in nursing homes.

Below are ten of the major running injuries. If you're having pain in a specific area that you think is caused by your running, look at the accompanying anatomical illustration to see if your pain matches any of the areas indicated on the illustration. Then read the appropriate description, and see if that sounds like what you're suffering. If it is, and your pain isn't restricting you in your daily, nonrunning activities, try the at-home treatments offered. I've asked around within the community of elite and former elite runners to find those who have had these injuries and successfully conquered them at home. This is not to say that you should automatically rule out seeing a sports medicine professional, but many low-grade running injuries can be beaten with a bit of tweaking and some hope and perseverance.

Plantar Fasciitis

WHERE IT HURTS: You'll feel pain along the inside bottom of your foot anywhere from the heel through the arch. Often the pain will be worst first thing in the morning when you step out of bed. It can also be especially bad after you've been sitting for a long time. It may lessen with walking or running.

WHAT IT IS: The plantar fascia is a fibrous band of tissue that connects your heel to your toes along the bottom of your foot. When your heel strikes the ground, the pressure on the heel can pull on the plantar fascia and can irritate and inflame the band.

WHY YOU GET IT: Two types of feet are more susceptible to plantar fasciitis: high-arched, rigid feet and flat feet. In the rigid foot, the plantar fascia is tighter than it should be as it spans the heel and toes. When you run, the bottom of your heel is jarred; this can inflame a tighter plantar fascia. Flat feet tend to overpronate (roll in too much after footstrike) more easily. Excessive pronation can pull it beyond its desirable range of motion.

HOW TO TREAT IT: I developed this in my early 40s. It took me a year and a half to conquer, and it remains the worst injury of my career. I tried a number of remedies: ibuprofen, stretching, icing, massage and wearing an elastic bandage as an arch support. Everything helped, but the arch support was the single most effective method of treatment. I've since discovered that keeping my calves less tight translated to more flexibility in my Achilles tendons and plantar fascia. I loosen my calves with 10 minutes of stretching after I run, I get an hour's massage every week and when my training and racing is heaviest, I go to the local pond to kick my legs and keep them loose. So far, this program has worked.

HOW TO PREVENT IT: The right shoes can be your best defense. If you have high-arched, rigid feet, select shoes with a good deal of cushioning and flexibility. This will allow for less pulling on the plantar fascia as your foot goes through its gait. If you have flat feet, you should seek medial support (extra stability along the inside heel). This limits the pulling of the fascia by keeping your foot in a more level position and not allowing too much inward roll. If you wear orthotics, the same principles apply; softer and more flexible for rigid feet, firmer and more supportive for flat feet. Other tips: if you've had plantar fasciitis, don't step out of bed barefoot. Put on thick socks or plush slippers first. Also, tight calves can require the plantar fascia to work harder than it's designed to. Work on your calf flexibility until you can bend your foot toward the front of your leg 10 degrees beyond a right angle.

Stress Fractures of the Foot

WHERE IT HURTS: Stress fractures of the foot are most likely to occur in the metatarsals or toe bones. You may ignore the pain at first, because it usually starts out as just a slight twinge. But if the condition goes unchecked, it can grow to be excruciating and put you out of running for a long time. Swelling is likely, and the area will be very sensitive. Even putting on a shoe can be very painful.

WHAT IT IS: Like muscles, bones break down so they can rebuild and come back stronger. Because of the pounding of running, tiny cracks can develop in weakened bones trying to rebuild. If you try to train through it and never give the bones time to mend, the cracks may become bigger and more painful. Eventually, they can even become a complete fracture.

WHY YOU GET IT: The pounding of running produces stress on the bones. Slapping against blacktop thousands of times a day or wearing improper footwear adds to this stress. Lightweight racing flats or other thin-soled shoes don't offer much protection and should be worn only occasionally. Increasing mileage too rapidly doesn't allow the bones the proper time to rebuild and can facilitate the condition.

HOW TO TREAT IT: Two of the best marathoners in American history have had this problem. Frank Shorter, the 1972 Olympic gold medalist and 1976 Olympic silver medalist, found that complete rest worked best for him. "I just stayed off my feet for three weeks," he says. Alberto Salazar, who won the New York City Marathon from 1980–1982 and the Boston Marathon in 1982, didn't have to miss as much running. "I've had this four times," Alberto says, "and I was able to train through it, with perhaps only ten days total off from running by doing a couple things. First, I modified my orthotics so as to shift the pressure away from the stress fracture. This has to be done carefully so that it doesn't cause a new injury. Second, I cut my mileage significantly—by more than 50 percent. Third, when I ran outdoors, I ran on soft but smooth and firm surfaces, such as good grass or a packed woodchip trail. Fourth, I took extra vitamins to help the bones heal. Fifth, I did as much of my running as possible on a treadmill set at an incline to lessen the pounding. And I would ice immediately after running and throughout the day would take anti-inflammatories for the tissues surrounding the bones."

HOW TO PREVENT IT: Choosing the proper footwear is essential. When your shoes feel significantly less cushioned or supportive, it's time for a new pair. Heed warning signs and run on softer surfaces when possible. Most important, give the bones time to recover and strengthen. Include calcium in your diet for bones to rebuild with.

Achilles Tendinitis

WHERE IT HURTS: You may feel anything from a burning sensation to sharp pain in the area from an inch above your heel to just below your calf muscle. It may be more severe when climbing stairs or changing directions.

WHAT IT IS: The Achilles tendon connects the heel to the calf muscles. It works in conjunction with the calf to pull the back of the foot up and allow for toe-off while running. It is a cord-like structure that has a fairly limited range of motion. If it's constantly forced to stretch past its normal length, it can become inflamed, or even rupture.

WHY YOU GET IT: The two main causes are excessive pronation and tight calf muscles. When your foot pronates too far, it pulls the tendon down, stretching it farther than it may have the capability to extend. If your calf muscles are too tight, the tendon is pulled again. When the heel is down, the distance between the calf and the back of the heel is greatest. If the calf muscles stay balled up, the Achilles is forced to lengthen itself more than it should. People with ultra-sensitive Achilles can have problems simply because the back of their shoe sits too high on the heel. This pressure on the tendon can cause pain.

HOW TO TREAT IT: Don Kardong, fourth in the 1976 Olympic Marathon, says, "I would always advise someone with Achilles tendinitis to try a heel lift. Put one in each shoe, for balance. I've had Achilles soreness a number of times, and this has always solved it." Adds Johnny Kelley, the two-time winner of the Boston Marathon and the record holder for the most completed Bostons (58!), "I would put soft, spongy rubber in both street and running shoes, and I would run on the grass until it was all better."

HOW TO PREVENT IT: Think of your Achilles tendon as a car engine—it needs time to warm up for top performance. When the blood is flowing more readily to the tendon, it's more resilient and less likely to give you trouble. If you overpronate, wear supportive shoes to keep your feet in a more neutral position. Stretch your calves regularly to keep them long and loose.

Gastrocnemius Strain/Pull

WHERE IT HURTS: Pain ranges from a little bit of soreness to excruciating pain and loss of use of the muscle. The gastrocnemius, better known as the calf, will feel tight and sore especially at toe-off or when you're climbing stairs or a hill. It may also be painful to the touch.

WHAT IT IS: The stiffness you feel after a hard run is a minor muscle strain. Muscles work by lengthening and contracting. When the fibers that make up the muscle are lengthened too far, you have a muscle pull or strain. If the action is very exaggerated and severe, the fibers can tear.

WHY YOU GET IT: If a muscle hasn't been properly warmed up and loosened, it's far more likely to be strained. Pushing off hard with your toes, as when you do speed work, makes your calves do extra work. So does running uphill or in shoes with a lower heel, such as road racing flats or track spikes. A calf muscle that's forced to extend and contract rapidly before sufficient blood flow has primed it for exercise will likely be strained or torn. Increasing the amount or intensity of an activity can also lead to muscle strains, causing muscles to work harder (extend and contract further) than they've been trained to do.

HOW TO TREAT IT: "For chronic calf pulls," says Don Kardong, "I would not advise self help. Find a good massage therapist with an underlying sadistic streak, and ask him or her to do deep tissue, cross fiber massage. I'm convinced it's the only solution." Johnny Kelley concurs. "When I was in the army, in 1942 or '43," he says, "I had a very bad calf. It was awful. I met a soldier who had a strong pair of hands and massaged away the problem using Vicks rub."

HOW TO PREVENT IT: The primary precaution is to prime the muscles for the activity. If you've been sitting around all day, don't suddenly launch into furious activity. Warm up and stretch the calf before hard runs. If your calves are sore, slow down and try to avoid running uphill. Because muscles work in pairs, if you strengthen the complementary muscles to the calf (those in the front of the shin), your legs will be better balanced. If these muscles are strong, they won't permit the calf to extend too far as easily.

Tibial Stress Syndrome (Shin Splints)

WHERE IT HURTS: Pain occurs on the shin or along the inside part of the lower leg, depending on whether it is a posterior or anterior shin splint. You'll feel pain when your foot strikes the ground or your toes are pulled toward your knee. The area may be tender to the touch.

WHAT IT IS: Shin splints are tiny tears of the muscles away from the tibia (shin bone). The area around the shin may become inflamed, or lumps may form where the muscle tries to reattach itself.

WHY YOU GET IT: There are many ways for shin splints to develop. Pronation and subsequent flattening of the arch is a common cause. The muscles in the shin help to hold up the arch, which, if it's continuously flattening, will eventually cause the tiny tears. The anterior shin muscles help take the shock of running and can tear if your shoes don't have adequate cushioning. As with many other injuries, muscle imbalances can lead to the condition. Stronger, tighter calf muscles that don't allow for a full range of motion in the shin muscles can cause injury, as can running on your toes all the time. Toe-running means the calves are constantly contracted and the opposing shin muscles are always extended; this can cause the tiny tears.

HOW TO TREAT IT: Ice your shins after running. Stay away from uphills and uneven surfaces. Loop a strap around a 5-pound weight, then loop that over your forefoot where your foot connects to your ties. Sit on the edge of a bed or table with your foot parallel to the floor and do toe raises. Start with two to three sets of 8 repetitions. Work up to three sets of 12.

HOW TO PREVENT IT: Proper shoes with good support to protect against overpronation and good cushioning can help ward off the malady, as can running on softer surfaces like grass. Stretching the calves and strengthening the shins is another proactive approach to defend against shin splints.

Iliotibial Band Syndrome

WHERE IT HURTS: The pain can occur in two places. Usually, you feel pain on the outside of your knee. But a tight iliotibial band can sometimes be felt along the outside of your hip. The discomfort may be sporadic—one day, you'll be fine, and the next you can hardly walk—and tends to recur after you've run a set distance.

WHAT IT IS: The iliotibial band is a thick cord that runs from the pelvis to the outside of the thigh and connects just below the knee. It stabilizes your thigh muscles and knee when you're running. As you run, the band glides over bone in your leg. If the band becomes too short and tight, the rubbing can cause the bursa (tiny sacs for lubrication) to become inflamed, or the band may become irritated.

WHY YOU GET IT: Bowlegged people are susceptible to this condition; their iliotibial band must be a little longer to compensate for the increased angle of their legs from the hip to knee. Running on uneven surfaces can also cause extra stress on the band. If the band is chronically tight and short, it's far more likely to scrape across the bone.

HOW TO TREAT IT: When it hits, it's too late. Cut your mileage to under the amount at which your pain starts. Stretch the band by crossing one leg behind the other and extending the opposite arm against the wall. Lean against the wall by pushing your opposite hip away from the wall. Hold for 5 seconds and do this 10 times. Repeat the stretch for the other band. Craig Masback, a 3:52 miler, says, "I'm convinced that there is no treatment for the injury—you just have to keep it from happening. Don't overtrain, don't run hills on very soft ground, and keep stretching. Anecdotal evidence tells me that people who have a problem with their iliotibial band show that problem early and have it often. Just as this injury was my first one as a high school sophomore, so was it my only significant injury when I was world class."

HOW TO PREVENT IT: Stretch and lengthen the iliotibial band. Make sure to stretch the whole band, both by the knee and hip. Run on even surfaces. Strengthening your groin muscles can help to keep your leg from swinging too far inward and placing more duress on the band. Also, if your quadriceps are weak, the iliotibial band will have to work harder. Straight leg raises will strengthen your thigh muscles.

Chondromalacia Patella (Runner's Knee)

WHERE IT HURTS: The pain is felt around and sometimes behind the knee cap. You might hear a crunching or clicking sound when you bend or extend your knee, and the discomfort may increase when you climb stairs.

WHAT IT IS: Runner's knee is caused by the softening and wearing away of the cartilage underneath the patella (knee cap). The patella has a tracking that it slides along during the running motion. When the patella is taken out of this tracking by moving side to side, the bones of the leg can rub against and roughen the cartilage of the knee. The rubbing and rougher texture of the cartilage cause the pain.

WHY YOU GET IT: There are two primary causes, which are also the causes of many other injuries: excessive pronation and muscle imbalance. If you overpronate, your lower leg tilts inward, and the patella is taken out of its normal tracking. Thigh muscles also help to align the knee cap and keep it straight. If the muscles in your thigh aren't up to par, they may not be able to help the knee guide itself along its proper course.

HOW TO TREAT IT: Ice any sore spots. Avoid running steep downhills and uneven surfaces.

HOW TO PREVENT IT: If you're a pronator, a good, medially supportive pair of shoes may be the gift that keeps your patella happy. Doing leg extensions is a good way to help the muscles in the front of the thigh grow stronger and better assist the patella in staying on track.

Hamstring Strain/Pull

WHERE IT HURTS: The muscles in the back of the leg, known as the hamstring, are attached by tendons to the pelvis and the thigh bone. Depending on where the strain or pull is, you're likely to feel pain at one of three sites: under the buttocks where they insert in the pelvis, deep in the back of your leg, or just above the back of your knee.

WHAT IT IS: A strain or pull is a tearing of the muscle or its connecting tendons. If all you feel is a little soreness or stiffness, the tears may only be microscopic. At the other end of the spectrum, you may not be able to put any weight on the afflicted leg because the pain is so great. This may indicate that the hamstring has been completely torn. A purplish-colored bruise may appear if the tearing is more severe.

WHY YOU GET IT: If you're like most people, you spend a good part of the day sitting, with your knees bent. This puts your hamstrings in a partially contracted position and can make them very tight. Many distance runners' quadriceps, the opposing muscle group of the hamstring, are overly developed. These stronger muscles injure the hamstring by straightening the leg with such force and speed that tears occur in the back of your leg. Frequent fast running, especially if you aren't warmed up properly, can increase your chances.

HOW TO TREAT IT: Jack Fultz, the winner of the 1976 Boston Marathon, says to keep stretching to a minimum while you have pain. "In stretching an injured muscle, as with many other aspects of training, less is more," he says. "I reduced my stretching to a minimum but continued to do very easy exercises for the area every day. If you can run without pain, but your hamstrings are still very tight, then slightly more aggressive stretching is probably warranted. Self-administered, cross fiber massage is something I used extensively to break up the adhesions at the top of my hamstrings. Press your fingers deeply into the belly of the muscle and roll the muscle like you're kneading bread dough. Do this perpendicular to the long fibers up and down your hamstrings." Adds Mark

Conover, the winner of the 1988 Olympic Marathon Trials, "I had this problem where the hamstring inserts just below the butt. My girlfriend would insert her fist into the area. She would do deep massage, almost Rolfing, to the area."

HOW TO PREVENT IT: A good warm-up can go a long way in preventing pulls. Gradual, easy stretching primes the muscle for the rigorous activity ahead and helps keep your muscles from becoming too short. Exercises to strengthen the hamstring, such as leg curls, can help deter tears from stronger quads. A looser, longer and stronger hamstring is far less likely to become torn.

Sciatica

WHERE IT HURTS: This one can be tough to diagnose because the sciatic nerve winds its way from the lower back, through the buttocks and down the backs of the legs. You may feel a dull ache along any of these points, and it may be difficult for you to pinpoint the exact location of the pain.

WHAT IT IS: The condition, which can be an enduring one, is caused by a strain on your sciatic nerve. This nerve bundle is a long chain of sensory receptors that follows a certain path down the lower half of your torso. If it's pushed off its route or comes in contact with something else along the way that pulls it off course, it can cause pain or numbness in the affected area. Because it covers so much distance in your body, it can be hard to nail down what's causing the pain.

WHY YOU GET IT: Misalignment of bone or ligament in the spine can tilt the nerve off course. If you have differences in your leg length, run on uneven surfaces or a posture that leans in one direction, your sciatic nerve is more vulnerable. These conditions can lead to pressure on the sciatic nerve and the resulting discomfort. Weak abdominal muscles can allow your spine to have a slight bend, which knocks the nerve off course again.

HOW TO TREAT IT: Watch your sitting posture—don't slump, because this causes extra pressure on your lower back. Take anti-inflammatories. When driving, keep a rolled towel under the affected leg where the hamstring inserts to the gluteal.

HOW TO PREVENT IT: Keep your lower back muscles loose with stretching; strengthen your abdominals with crunches. Try to run on level surfaces and maintain good posture throughout the day to keep the nerve bundle aligned.

Piriformis Syndrome

WHERE IT HURTS: The piriformis is a muscle in the hip that helps your hip to rotate. The pain can be in your upper leg or the buttocks, depending on where the limiting factor of your hip rotation comes from. The back section of the buttock on the outside may be sensitive to touch.

WHAT IT IS: The discomfort here can also come from the sciatic nerve. If your hips can't rotate properly, the piriformis muscle can become inflamed and swollen. Because the sciatic nerve runs beside the piriformis, the swelling of the piriformis can cause pressure and inflammation of the sciatic nerve as well.

WHY YOU GET IT: The rotation of the hips isn't an easy job. Your lower back must work smoothly with your legs, especially the hamstrings. The lower back and hamstrings should be flexible, to allow for rotation. Tightness in the back or leg areas can make rotating your hip properly in either direction difficult. When the piriformis is working against the tightness in your back or legs, it can become inflamed.

HOW TO TREAT IT: Use pretty much the same treatment as for sciatica. Also, sit on a tennis ball where the pain is most severe during long car rides and plane trips.

HOW TO PREVENT IT: Like most injuries, stretch and strengthen. Make sure the lower back and upper leg allow for a full range of motion by doing stretches for your lower back and legs. You can make the muscles that rotate the hip stronger by lying face down, bending the leg at a 90 degree angle and gently raising the knee off the floor.

When to See a Doctor, and Who to See

Minor aches and pains are part of running, especially when you're starting out or trying to reach your potential. Almost all of us have our little sore spots that we've learned to live with, and in most cases, these are nothing to worry about if you consistently give them special care. My calves, for example, can become very tender, and since my bout with plantar fasciitis, I pay extra attention to them through stretching and continual evaluation.

An acute, new pain, however, is another matter. These are signals that something is off. The key to staying on top of injuries is to always be on the lookout for them, and to tend to them as soon as they begin to sprout. If your new ache subsides during your run, then it's okay to keep running, although you should cut back some in intensity and distance. Ice the area after your run, and again during the day. If the pain gets worse during your run, get home as soon as possible and ice. If you try to run the next day, stay close to home, and only return to your former mileage if, at the least, the pain doesn't increase when you run. If the pain makes you limp when you walk and doesn't ease during the day, don't run, but ice several times during the day. See a doctor if this state persists for more than a week. And if the pain occurs

WHEN TO ICE, WHEN TO HEAT

Runners are often told to ice their injuries, but sometimes we hear that heat is the way to go. Which should you use (and when) to best treat and beat your injuries?

Start by understanding what happens in a typical running injury. The tissues of a muscle, tendon or ligament are damaged by overuse, by being stretched beyond their breaking point or by the repeated pounding of hitting the ground with at least three times your body weight, thousands of times per run. Blood vessels tear, and there's swelling. The greater the swelling, the more severe the injury is, and the longer recovery will take. That's why it's crucial to tend immediately to the slightest flare-up.

Your immediate goal, then, is to reduce that swelling. Do this with ice. Cold causes blood vessels to constrict, so bleeding into the injured tissues slows, and swelling decreases. The damaged tissue relaxes; this not only decreases pain, but also slows the injured tissue's metabolism, so there's less tissue breakdown.

If you apply heat at this point, you'll make things worse. Applied warmth increases blood flow to an area, and this is exactly the opposite of what a damaged tissue needs, because that will increase its swelling. Damaged tissues have different needs from those that are merely tight. Generalized soreness responds well to heat and stretching, but more localized pain means a strain or a micro-tear. These latter need ice.

Heat is best used once your inflammation is gone. This usually takes at least 72 hours. With the increased blood flow to an area that heat causes, more oxygen is going to and more waste products are being removed from the damaged area. If your swelling has decreased noticeably, but you still have a little inflammation, alternate heat and ice after a few days of ice-only treatment. Heat the area for a few minutes, then ice it for the same amount of time. Do this for 15 to 20 minutes. Stretch the hurt area for 5 minutes, then repeat the contrast treatment.

A great way to ice is with paper cups that you've frozen water in. The cup allows your hand to stay warm while you're applying the ice, and you can put the cup back in the freezer for the next session when you're done. Rub in circular motions for at least 5 minutes; 15 to 20 minutes would be better. The area should become red and numb, not white and numb. When I'm fighting inflammation, I try to ice the injured area a few times throughout the day in addition to when I've just finished running. Another old trick is to use an application that will mold around your injured area, such as a bag of frozen vegetables.

If you're heating an area, a heating pad is an obvious choice. Most sports medicine professionals recommend that you not heat an area for more than 20 minutes at a time because of the possibility of mild skin burn. As with ice, heat's effectiveness is increased if you repeat the treatment throughout the day. When you use heat to warm up before a workout, 5 to 10 minutes is plenty.

even when you're sitting or standing, immediately seek professional help.

If you do need professional help, who should you see? That depends on where you hurt. Here are some general guidelines for the areas in which runners are most often injured.

Foot and Lower Leg

These can be treated by orthopedists or osteopaths, but they're most often treated by podiatrists, who will have the designation "D.P.M." (doctor of podiatric medicine) following their name. Podiatrists complete 4 years of training at a college of podiatric medicine and a residency. Their training focuses on feet and feet-related problems. They are licensed to perform surgery and prescribe medicine. They're valuable for runners to see, because they'll examine your biomechanics and determine if the way your feet move through the gait cycle is causing your pain. (Often, structural problems in the feet can lead to injury elsewhere.)

Knee

These are most often treated by orthopedic surgeons, although you can also see osteopaths or podiatrists. Orthopedists are medical doctors (M.D.s) who treat injuries to bones, muscles, tendons and ligaments. As a runner, it's important to find one who views surgery as a last resort to injury, not a panacea. Podiatrists often treat knee injuries with orthotics.

Thigh and Hip

These injuries are often seen by osteopaths or orthopedists. Osteopaths (D.O.s) are, like M.D.s, licensed to practice all branches of medicine and surgery. They're more likely, however, to view your injury systemically and try to determine if there's a structural cause to your problem, either at the injured site or in another body part that affects the injured part. This makes osteopaths a good choice for runners who are interested in attacking the cause, not the symptom.

If your running friends can't recommend a good specialist in these fields, contact the following organizations to find one in your area:

Orthopedists: American Orthopedic Society for Sports Medicine; (708) 292–4900

Osteopaths: American Osteopathic Academy of Sports Medicine; (608) 831–4400

Podiatrists: American Academy of Podiatric Sports Medicine; (301) 424–7440

CROSSTRAINING

When I first heard the word "crosstraining" several years ago, I didn't like it. It seemed as if running was being denigrated, considered one of any number of equivalent activities. I'm happy to admit that I was wrong. Now I have a better understanding of what crosstraining for runners means, and I realize that I've always done it.

I classify crosstraining activities for runners into two groups—strengthening exercises and aerobic alternatives. I'm all in favor of any activity that you want to use to supplement your running; for nonracers especially, I really like the idea of doing more than one thing. Don't we all prefer a life with a good amount of variety? That said, I'm going to concentrate on strengthening exercises. By now, most people know many ways to work out aerobically, and most people accept that everybody, not just high-paid jocks, should regularly do this type of exercise. Strengthening exercises, however, are still considered mainly the domain of bodybuilders and football players. That's too bad. Being stronger helps your running in so many ways, and, performance aside, decent muscular strength is crucial for maintaining a high quality of life as you age.

As I said, I now realize I've been crosstraining on a low-key basis pretty much since I began to run. In high school, regular calisthenics were part of our daily routine. We would do push-ups, sit-ups, chin-ups—anything that we could do using the resistance of our body weight that would build overall strength. We also lifted dumbbells and jumped rope. All runners, but especially young runners and beginners, should do some sort of the same. These exercises are easy to do and effective. It's the wear and tear injuries that get to you as a distance runner, so if your muscles and connective tissues are strong, they'll hold up better. Also, many running injuries are compensatory ones—you're weak in one part, and another body part has to pick up the slack and can be asked to do more than it's designed for. For example, if your quadriceps are weak, then your iliotibial band, which helps your quadriceps extend your leg as you run, will have to work harder, and it may become so inflamed that you won't be able to run. Young runners who compete on their school's team are often immediately thrown into regular hard running, both in training and with frequent racing. The stronger their bodies are, the better they can withstand this less-than-ideal introduction to the sport.

Once I was out of college and started running again in the early '70s, I resumed lifting weights. I've done pretty much the same program since then. It's certainly nothing fancy, and I'm sure I could have done more, especially when I was trying to be the best in the world, but I've always liked knowing that I'm doing a good, low-key workout that I can easily incorporate into my routine. I have 12-pound dumbbells. Twice a week, I do two sets of basic exercises—curls, presses, etc. When I was at my peak, knowing that I was doing this consistently gave me a big psychological boost, because I would tell myself that it was just one more area of my training that I was taking care of that perhaps others I would be racing against were neglecting. You can get the same boost over your competitors, and it only takes about 30 minutes a week. I also do 50 sit-ups and 12 push-ups a day. Again, this takes almost no time.

Obviously, others have much more intense strengthening programs, and you might benefit from one, but then it's also easier to go over the edge, or doing it becomes so involved that you're more likely to miss it. I've never been one who lives to train. Strength training is just another example of the point I keep trying to make—cover all your bases pretty well on a consistent basis and don't obsess over every little detail. You're more likely to improve and to do well over the long haul with this approach.

At the other extreme, there are those who say distance runners shouldn't do any strengthening work. These people argue that if muscular strength were a requirement to running well, then your regular running would develop it. I have two problems with this argument. First, the demands of racing are very different from the changes your body undergoes through regular, steady state running. When you're pushing to your limits, you need all the help you can get. As a distance runner, if you're stronger, then you're better able to get through the long workouts that are necessary to race well. For example, if your back, shoulders and stomach are strong, then you can maintain good running posture longer once you start to tire. Your form won't deteriorate, and, with your chest remaining erect rather than slumped, you can maintain normal breathing better. It's all about making the racing easier. My second point is more subjective. I know I felt more capable of running marathons at 5:00 per mile when I was consistent with my low-key program. Maybe I was deluding myself, but I did win the Boston and New York City Marathons four times each, so something was working.

As I've aged, I've realized my strengthening routine has great benefits independent of helping me to race well. The main one is that it slows, if not stops, the loss of muscle mass that occurs with age. Studies have consistently shown that if you continue to occasionally overload your muscles as you age, you can maintain nearly all of the muscular strength you had in your 20s and 30s. It's become a cliché, but muscular strength and aging is the ultimate example of use it or lose it. Moreover, studies conducted on sedentary people in their 80s have found that you can recover great amounts of strength no matter what your age or how long you've been away from a regular strengthening program. In one study, women in their 80s nearly tripled their strength in just more than a month!

Why should you care about strength training as you age? Simply because your life will be better if you do, no matter how aerobically fit you are. In addition to maintaining your muscles and connective tissues, regular, moderate strengthening exercises help maintain bone density. Strong bones and strong muscles help older people maintain their autonomy and, therefore, their self-esteem. That's why although I began my strengthening work solely to race better, I'm now convinced that doing it should be a part of everyone's routine, whether you're ever going to race or not.

Aerobic Alternatives

I am first and foremost a runner, and I hope that I always will be. Even with the concessions that I've made to age, 95 percent of my training time is spent running. Why? For the simple reasons that it produces results for me, that I enjoy it and that I'm still able to run 70 to 90 miles per week consistently without breaking down.

So I'm not going to pretend that I'm an expert on the ever-increasing array of aerobic alternatives that are out there. (Let's just say that it would take a lot for me to put on a pair of in-line skates.) I've used exercise bikes and rowing machines to try to maintain some fitness (and sanity!) when I've been injured, but have never systematically used any other aerobic alternative to supplement my running. Also, I'm not an indoor exerciser; I've yet to go to a fitness club on a regular basis. For example, I'd much rather cycle outdoors than on a stationary bike. I have a treadmill in my basement, but, to be honest, its main use is as a fort of sorts for my younger daughter. Running outside is what it's all about.

Again, I'm fortunate enough to be able to run enough to race at the level that I want. Many runners, of course, can't run beyond a certain amount without getting injured or stale. If you're one of them, and have seen your performances plateau, then you could definitely benefit from finding a complementary activity to help build your aerobic base. You still have to focus on the running if you want to race well, but as long as you maintain that focus, adding to your repertoire is only going to make you a healthier, fitter person.

You might also find yourself enjoying your running more. My wife, Gail, used to run marathons. Now she does just about every fitness activity imaginable, and although she's running less, she's appreciating it more. Now, running is a fun part of a well-rounded program for her, not an obligation.

Teens and masters can especially benefit from a variety of crosstraining activities. Teens because young runners should concentrate on developing overall body fitness, and masters because crosstraining helps maintain muscle mass lost with age and, like I said, allows more injury-free aerobic training than might be possible if you rely on running alone. As with my recommendations on strength training, diet and nearly everything else, experiment to find what's going to work most easily given your schedule. Many runners report satisfaction with stair machines. But if it takes you a few hours a week just to get to one, you're not as likely to stick with it and benefit from it as you might from, say, an exercycle in your home, even if you like the stair machine better. If you can afford to, I recommend buying a piece of equipment for your home if a health club isn't convenient and if you know that you're going to use the equipment consistently. Yes, they can be expensive, but how do you quantify the supreme feeling of being fit?

I hate to discourage any runner from trying any useful activity. Still, if I had to pick one supplementary activity that will help you the most as a runner, it would be swimming, because it has so many benefits. We know it can be a great upper body strengthener—something we runners are often notoriously good at avoiding. As I said, I've especially felt the value of such upper body work as I've gotten older.

When I swim, I don't do much—about 15 to 20 minutes of varying strokes. That's a minimum to strengthen my arms and shoulder and back muscles. I also like to swim for relaxation and for the cooling effect. I always take this time to float on my back and just let the run's fatigue melt away. Kicking your legs is terrific for loosening tight tendons and muscles in your feet, ankles and legs. I have successfully fought off Achilles tendinitis by kicking my legs in a pool for 10 to 15 minutes after a run.

Finally, there's an element to a well-rounded program that we runners are notorious for overlooking—rest. As I age, I continually make adjustments in my training to be sure I'm incorporating enough rest. This can get very tricky; after all, I've never gotten old before. Knowing how much to rest rather than train is guesswork, but I have the sense that if I got in a good run in the morning and I don't have any important races coming up, then I'm better off resting than heading out for a short run or cycling for 40 minutes. I still

make mistakes, mostly because I used to be able to get away with so much. For example, when I won the New York City Marathon in 1976, I ran 141 miles the week that ended 4 days before the race, and I always trained through shorter races without even a hint of a taper. (Once I almost set a 5K PR in an evening race after running 15 miles in the morning.) Now, I run an easy 3 miles the day before a race, and I try to make the day before that a short and easy run, too. I've made similar adjustments with rest during my normal training week, and I'll continue to do so, and to alter the mix of running and crosstraining that I do, as I move into my 50s and beyond.

STRETCHING

As with diet, stretching is one of those areas in which you're most likely to encounter zealots, both pro and con. Some people swear that an intricate, daily stretching ritual is the only thing that keeps them alive, much less running. On the other hand, some runners think stretching is an invitation to injury, and avoid it like they do cigars. As usual, I fall somewhere in between.

If you're a runner, you should stretch. Keeping your muscles, tendons and ligaments resilient will help you enjoy your running more, whether that means feeling good on a specific run or maintaining a range of motion that will allow you to train and race as hard as you want. At the same time, stretching isn't the key to running well—as I keep emphasizing, running is—yet there are runners who spend more time stretching than they do running. Your stretching routine should be just one more thing, such as wearing good running shoes, eating healthfully, etc., that you get in the habit of doing simply because it makes your running easier and, therefore, better.

My current approach to stretching is the same one I've had pretty much my whole career. As you may have guessed by now, it's neither extensive nor revolutionary. I try to stretch every day for 10 to 15 minutes, and, as often as possible, I stretch soon after finishing a run. Studies have shown this is the best time to stretch—your muscles are warmed up, there's less of a risk of injuring yourself by straining too far, and you're more likely to be relaxed. It can be very soothing to finish a run, get something to drink, change into dry clothes, and spend 15 minutes gently stretching the muscles you've just exercised. On my best days, I think of stretching afterward as an extension of my run. It's a great time to reflect on the run you've just finished, to think about your future training or racing or to continue to clear your mind from the stress of the workaday world. When it's hot, and I'm not short on time, sometimes I stretch a bit right after a run, then drive to a pool. There, I'll swim for 10 minutes or so to cool off and relax, then I'll do some kicking in the water for another 10 minutes. This helps keep me loose, and it's a nice treat to look forward to when I'm out there running in the heat.

I'm pretty good at procrastinating, though, and sometimes I don't allow myself enough time after a run to get in some good stretching before I have to jump in the shower and dash off somewhere. In those instances, I try to find another short block of time later in the day to stretch. For example, I'll sit on the floor and stretch for 10 minutes while watching television. I know it's not ideal, and I know I shouldn't try to stretch as far as when my muscles are warmer after a run, but it's better than nothing.

This is an example of another key point of running for a lifetime—you're more likely to succeed in the long run if you keep a flexible approach (no pun intended) rather than an all-or-nothing outlook. So you got home from work late, and really don't have time to run for an hour and stretch for 15 minutes afterward as you planned? OK, what's the best you can make of your changed situation? Can you run for half an hour and maybe stretch a bit in the shower and after eating dinner? My point is that giving yourself just one definition of success can be self-defeating. Do what you can, and emphasize the positives in that.

Sometimes I stretch a little before starting a moderate training run. For example, if I've raced the day before, and my calves feel tighter or sorer than usual, I'll gently lean into a wall for a few minutes before starting my run. (I'll also start my run more slowly than on days when I don't have specific aches.) Don't worry about doing too much in these instances, though. The best way to loosen a tight muscle is to gently increase the range of motion through which you work it; 10 minutes of easy running will more effectively eliminate some of that tightness than 10 minutes of stretching.

I always stretch before running hard, whether in a speed workout or a race. For both, I have the same routine. I stretch my lower back, Achilles tendons, calves and hamstrings for a minute or two each, then do a 2-mile warm-up jog. Then I stretch for a few minutes while I'm loose, and then change into my racing shoes. (I wear them during speed work, too. See the section on shoes in Chapter 2.) Once I have my racing shoes on, I do some 100-meter striders to loosen up even more and to see if I'm warmed up enough for the greater range of motion that running fast requires. I allow myself enough time before a race to stretch more if I still feel tight while I'm doing striders.

If I'm doing an interval workout and I start feeling tight enough in a certain area that it's interfering with my workout, I'll stop and stretch, then resume the workout. I know that the extra minute or two between hard efforts doesn't compromise the quality of the workout too much; to the extent that it does, I'd rather have to deal with that than with an injury brought on by ignoring some pain that began during a workout.

I can't recommend a universally applicable stretching routine. I've found the stretches that hit the areas that I have the most problems with, and you should do the same. Most runners are going to want to stretch the muscles and tendons along the back of their bodies, because these become shorter and tighter with distance running if you don't tend to them. This includes your Achilles tendons, calves, hamstrings, gluteals and lower back. The running magazines regularly exhibit the standard stretches for these areas, and there are also any number of books that do an excellent job of displaying many stretches for key body parts. Try these basics, but don't be afraid to experiment with modifying them to better reach your tightest and sorest spots.

For example, my Achilles tendons and calves are amongst my most troublesome body parts. I do some of the typical stretches for these areas, such as wall push-ups, but I've also found some not-so-standard ways to keep them loose. I like to lie on my back and pull my legs back or put them straight up in the air. I can feel the blood flow down through my legs. Then I shake my calves and ankles, and do rotations in the air with my feet. The ankle is that lever that you're pushing off of with every strike, so you always want to be taking care of it. Again, I'm not saying mine is the only way, but give this routine a try, and then see if you can find a way to alter it to suit your needs.

I've learned how to do more stretches that work for me out of necessity. As I've aged, but especially in the last 3 or 4 years, I've had to become more knowledgeable and more consistent about stretching. Most masters runners will find this to be the case. You may not be training as intensely as you once did—I know I'm not—but you're still putting in a solid effort, and what used to be an easy week in terms of mileage now counts as a hard week. If you can get yourself to stretch for 10 to 15 minutes, 4 times a week, the miles will come easier to you. The slowing ability to spring back from a hard effort is likely to be one of the first major changes you'll notice when you pass the age of 40; as a master, you need always to be thinking about how best you can recover from one workout to be ready for the next.

The minimal investment of time I'm recommending you give to stretching—just one hour out of the 168 in a week—will pay big returns. You'll feel better immediately after a run, you'll feel better the next day, you'll maintain your range of motion, and your daily running will be easier. Remember, one of the main goals of running for a lifetime is to avoid injury. Consistent, moderate stretching will keep your muscles, tendons and ligaments better able to handle what you ask of them, and less likely to balk when you want to run farther or faster than usual.

At the same time, young runners should also be especially good about stretching regularly. High school running often involves a lot of fast running right from the start of the season. Teens' connective tissues are definitely more resilient than those of, say, their parents who run, but that doesn't mean that they're immune to injury. The heavy amount of speed work and racing that are part of most high school programs requires young bodies to continually work through an extended range of motion. It's important that their muscles, tendons and ligaments, which usually don't have years of running in the bank to strengthen them, be prepared. When I'm doing lots of speed work and racing frequently, I'm especially careful about stretching. Given that this is what teen runners are always doing, they should be, too.

MASSAGE

There are many reasons why I've been able to run for so long, race so much and seldom get injured—good genes, consistency in my training and knowing when to back off and when to push, among others. But one of the major factors in my longevity is one of the most underrated. Since 1980, I've been getting an hour's massage once a week. Other than paying for good running shoes, this is the best financial investment in your running that you can make.

You've probably seen news reports about people whose cars last for phenomenal numbers of miles. These cases aren't flukes—usually the owners check the oil nearly daily, get regular tune-ups, and are equally fastidious about other areas of maintenance and upkeep. That's how I think about my weekly massage. I'm always telling my friends who aren't top runners that they can get as great, if not greater, benefits from it as I do, especially if they're running longer races. It's worth that $40 a week. You're investing in yourself and in your good health. How can you place a financial value on the importance of feeling good and enjoying your running? I recognize that some people's budgets just won't allow regular massages, but for most runners, it's laziness and lack of belief in the continual benefits that keep them from going. All I can tell you is that I've been training and racing hard for 30 years and I can still run to the level that I want; I think that my weekly massages are one of the top reasons why. I really feel the effects the next day, but by now I've come to discern them long after. And let's not forget the psychological benefits of being relaxed, of having stress relieved and of knowing that you're taking good care of yourself, and in a very enjoyable way.

I've been going to the same massage therapist for the past 5 years. Before that, I went to a different person for 5 years. Once you find someone you feel comfortable working with, stick with that person. You two can get to know each other, and a good therapist will become increasingly proficient at addressing your neediest spots and at noticing how you're faring from week to week. This is why I'm not a big advocate of the post-race massages that are offered at many events. It may feel good, and the person working on you may be qualified, but he or she doesn't know you and might work too hard on you. After a long race, your muscles are going to be especially sore and tender, and therefore vulnerable if subjected to an unaccustomed treatment. It's a much better idea to schedule a massage for later that day or the next day with your regular therapist.

How do you find a good massage therapist? The best way is to ask around. I had heard about my current therapist through another runner whose judgment I trust, so I thought that she was worth giving a try. Five years later, she obviously was. Don't have qualms about shopping around, though. Before finding my current therapist, I saw a number of people after my prior long-time therapist had moved away. After we had worked together weekly for 5 years, it was natural that seeing others would be a letdown; still, after about five sessions, I could tell that I just wasn't getting the benefits I wanted out of our sessions, even though I communicated what I wanted done. So I tried my current therapist, and we were a much better fit. She's a runner; this really helps her help me. You don't necessarily have to find a runner, but your therapist should at least be used to working with athletes. There's a big difference between the general relaxation massage that sedentary people indulge in occasionally and the goal-oriented, deep-tissue nature of sport massage. When investigating therapists, ask if they regularly work with athletes. You want someone who is going to understand why you're there and who can do something about it. Compared to 20 years ago, there are many more therapists who are used to working with athletes and who know that we need a different kind of treatment than sedentary people. A good starting point is to find someone who has been certified by the American Massage Therapy Association.

My therapist spends the bulk of our hour together working on my hamstrings and calves. These are my most tender spots, and they likely will be yours, too. Sometimes she'll work on my lower back, shoulders and neck, and although this work feels very good and is relaxing, that's not the main reason I'm there. If I've been fighting a sore hamstring, and I tell my therapist that I'd like her to focus her attention there, she will. That's the kind of communication you want to establish.

As a runner, you want deep-tissue massage. Your therapist should really be digging into those muscles, rather than just gently working the surface. You should feel that your therapist is really working on an area. Don't be alarmed by a little discomfort, but you don't want acute pain. Again, it's important the two of you be able to communicate. If you tell your therapist to work harder or easier on an area, and you're ignored, it's time to find someone new. It's your body and enjoyment of your running that we're talking about here.

Joan Benoit Samuelson

In 1979, Joan Benoit and I wore hats while setting course records to win the Boston Marathon. Since then, Joan has seen her life change often, including adopting her married name of Samuelson. One thing, though, has remained constant. "Life is going to go on," she says, "and I'm going to keep running."

Her running has taken many forms since she started as a ninth-grader in Cape Elizabeth, Maine. "I have two brothers who ran cross country," she remembers, "and I enjoyed watching them race, so I tried it." As was common in the early 1970s, Joan's school had no formal track team for women, and she had to settle for a club-system team that had formed. The lack of equality for women's running was bothersome, but not enough to discourage her. "I simply loved to run," Joan says. "We had some meets, so I was able to com-

pete. The longest event by my senior year was the mile, so naturally I wanted to try that." She not only tried, but won the state meet that year.

She also tried races beyond the mile on the track. "I ran road races in the summer in high school—10Ks, 10-milers," she says. "I liked the idea of challenging myself with longer and longer distances." This was much different from my high school experience; I usually ran just a few miles a day and certainly didn't run 10-mile road races. When I graduated, my longest run, race or not, was 12 miles. So you might think that, in hindsight, I'm against Joan's approach in her teens. Well, there are many ways to develop gradually, which is what I recommend as the best way for young runners to keep running past graduation and for a lifetime. Although her distances were longer than mine, this is just what Joan did.

"I think it's important to emphasize my introduction to running in ninth grade," she says. "I started because I wanted to, and I kept at it because I wanted to. And I wasn't too young. I think that intense age-group competition isn't all that good. I would have burned out on running if I had started too young and done that." I also don't think that Joan's program in her teens was misguided, because although she did run long road races during the summer, she put them aside during the school year and concentrated on the short track races. This allowed her to build a good speed base and to learn how to incorporate several types of training and racing into her program. That well-rounded approach has stayed with her throughout her running career. For example, just 2 months before setting a world record of 2:22:43 to win the 1983 Boston Marathon, Joan ran 4:36 for the mile at an indoor track race.

Joan continued to build her running intelligently in college, and she won the national cross country title during her senior year at Maine's Bowdoin College. The next winter, she ran her first marathon the day after running a 10K, and on what she had told friends would be a training run, ran 2:50. Three months later, wearing her Bowdoin singlet and a Boston Red Sox cap, she ran 2:35 to win the 1979 Boston Marathon in American-record time. After our victories there, Joan and I were invited to a White House dinner by President Carter. Quite an intelligent buildup, indeed.

You probably know about some of Joan's racing triumphs after that. She redefined women's marathoning with her 1983 Boston win, attacking the course with an aggressiveness not seen before, and she was rewarded with that 2:22 world record. In 1984, she scored an emotional victory at the Women's Olympic Marathon Trials just 17 days after arthroscopic surgery on her knee, pedaling an exercise bike with her arms in the days between surgery and the race to maintain her fitness. That summer, she bravely dashed from the field just 3 miles into the first Women's Olympic Marathon, and never looked back en route to a gold medal. And in the fall of 1985, Joan ran 2:21:21 at the Chicago Marathon to break her own American record. No other American woman has run within 5 minutes of that time.

Given all that, you might think she is some kind of otherworldly running machine. As I said, I'm fortunate enough to call Joan my friend, and can tell you otherwise. I hope that by now you've come to see I'm a runner just like you. I was blessed with the ability to run long distances fast, and I've worked very hard to nurture that talent, but that's ultimately incidental. I'm out there for a lifetime for the same fundamental reason as you: my life would be worse in so many ways if I wasn't. That's the same message that Joan, with all of her records and medals and accomplishments, has.

These days, as Joan nears her 40s, it's been awhile since her last 2:30 marathon. Since winning the Olympics and flirting with being the first woman under 2:20 in the marathon, Joan has shifted gears. Her husband, Scott, and her children, daughter Abby and son Anders, are now the focus of her life. (So much so that Joan laughingly divides her running into two phases: BC, or before children, and AD, or after delivery.) And, as happens to many runners after they have children, she's switched some of her considerable ability to concentrate on herself toward a wider view, not just toward her children, but also in a variety of community involvements.

"I look at my life, and it's a lot different now," Joan acknowledges. "There's the aspect of where my time and energy goes. It used to be almost all on my running. Now, it's the children. It's not that I don't concentrate on my running.

[Just 3 months before her 39th birthday, Joan ran 2:36:54 to place 13th at the 1996 Olympic Marathon Trials.] It's that I walk a fine line."

Her love of running remains unsullied. "Running is such a part of my life," she understates. "If I were never to run another marathon, I would still do two-hour runs. Running those loops brings back great memories. Those long runs cleanse my system, physically and mentally. Same thing with speed work. I like the challenge." Sound like anybody you know?

Joan and I differ in one major way. I'm constantly tweaking things, setting new race goals as I enter new age divisions. This is how I keep my running fresh and challenging. As she nears her 40s, Joan says that she won't do that.

"I'm not going to set any masters goals. I'm not going to do anything different just because I'm a certain age. I mean, I've certainly had to make adjustments—I've had some injuries and because of them and because of being a mother, I've changed biomechanically. And physically, I know I don't recover like I used to. But when people ask me about emphasizing racing as a master, I think, 'Another year or two years or ten years—who cares?' I'll always keep running as long as I can. Just like I hope to be a mother the rest of my life, I hope to be a runner the rest of my life."

Women's Running Section

FEATURING SPECIAL ADVICE FROM JOAN BENOIT SAMUELSON

Author's note: Almost all of the advice I have for you in this book comes from my 30-year career of trying whatever I thought might work to help me run faster and more enjoyably. That being the case, I can't speak from experience about the many topics that are of unique concern to women runners. I can, however, relate what I've learned by listening to and talking to thousands of women runners of a wide range of ability over the years.

Besides my wife, Gail, the woman whose advice on running I place most stock in is Joan Benoit Samuelson, who, in 1984, won the first Olympic Marathon for women. Joan and I have been close friends for more than 15 years. During that time, I've seen her make many adaptations in her running as her life has changed—she's gotten married, had two children and, like all of us, has had to figure out how to deal with running and aging.

I keep emphasizing the importance of figuring out how to make your running work for you given your current place in life. To me, few people show the ability to do this better than Joan. In this section, I offer advice about issues that are of special concern to women runners: female-specific disorders, nutrition, menstural cycles, pregnancy, birth control and the dangerous Female Athlete Triad. The information comes from various sources, most notably from extensive discussions with Joan Benoit Samuelson.

MENSTRUAL CYCLES

All runners are affected by cycles in their training, but none as potentially problematic as a woman's menstrual cycle. During the week or so before menstruation, many women report such symptoms as bloating, fatigue, irritability, mood swings and food cravings. The good news (if there is any) is that many women runners report that these symptoms are lessened by some form of aerobic exercise. Joan, for example, is susceptible to moodiness, but finds that persevering with her running, rather than giving in to her symptoms, improves her mood and releases some of her negative energy.

As with so many other aspects of your running, the key is to be adaptable and to make the most of the hand that you're dealt. That means readjusting your training goals for a few days, if necessary, and not beating yourself up about it. At the same time, it means doing what you can to maintain control of the situation, just as you would when you're injured. For example, many women runners are very conscious about their weight, and therefore try to resist the food cravings that can accompany their periods. This is often counterproductive, not only because if you do eventually give in to them, you're likely to overindulge, but also because these cravings can be a sign that your body needs more fuel.

According to Nancy Clark, M.S., R.D., who is a leading sports nutritionist, a woman's metabolic rate can increase significantly during the premenstrual period. Some women need as much as 500 extra calories a day during this time; that's the equivalent of five bananas or chocolate chip cookies, or more than two bagels. If you don't meet these extra needs while maintaining your usual training, your already-low energy will sag even more. In the same way, some women restrain their fluid intake during their period, because they already feel bloated enough, compared to their usual, leaner body image. But the bloating can be caused by sodium retention, meaning that drinking more, not less, fluid is the solution. More water will flush out that retained sodium and should lessen the bloating. As with denying your body the food it needs during your premenstrual time, being inadequately hydrated is only going to add to your fatigue and lessened enjoyment of running.

Although running has been shown to lessen many of the side effects of menstruation, it can increase the most visible sign, bleeding. Some of the painkillers that can help with symptoms, such as ibuprofen, also reduce bleeding. This is especially beneficial for women runners, because less bleeding means less iron loss, and, therefore, less chance of impaired performance. Still, it's reasonable to be concerned about visible bleeding while you're running. Fortunately, most women don't overflow when they run. If you do, adopt one of Joan's techniques, and run with a tampon in a plastic bag pinned inside of your shorts.

Your period's effects on your running is one matter. There's also the flip side of the issue to consider, namely, running's effects on your period. Some women find that running lightens and shortens their period and lengthens their cycle. This can be good. What's not good is when you lose your periods altogether. This is called amenorrhea, and although it might seem like a dream come true, it's dangerous. We'll look at it more closely in its relation to two other conditions discussed below.

THE FEMALE ATHLETE TRIAD

The Female Athlete Triad is a relatively new term in sports medicine. It exists because of a growing recognition of the interconnectedness of three potentially lethal conditions: disordered eating, amenorrhea and osteoporosis.

Disordered Eating

The first component of the Triad, disordered eating, encompasses a broad spectrum of problems, whose extremes are anorexia nervosa and bulimia. To have an eating disorder, however, a runner doesn't have to starve herself or constantly binge and purge. Most female runners, Clark notes, have more subtle forms of eating problems; she estimates that about 30 percent of female athletes have some sort of problem with food.

A runner may eat, Clark says, but may not eat enough to support the tremendous physical demands on her body. Numerous studies show, for example, that caloric intakes among highly trained female runners (those who average almost 90 miles per week), recreational female runners and sedentary women are similar, despite their very different energy needs. Among female runners, intakes are often consistently low—between 1,500 and 2,000 calories per day—even though these women may expend an additional 1,000 calories per day through training. Over the long haul, women who restrict caloric intake become "energy efficient": their bodies adapt to lower intakes by lowering their metabolic activity, Clark explains. This makes their self-restraint self-defeating. They eat less to try to keep their weight down. This lowers their metabolic rate, meaning they burn even fewer calories through daily living and exercise, when their goal is to stay lean. So by restricting their calories they cause their bodies to need fewer calories—their bodies rightfully go into starvation mode—and it becomes that much more difficult to stay lean. Plus, with restricted calories, they don't replace what they lose through training, and their performance becomes erratic.

Female runners also frequently exclude certain food groups, such as dairy products. Clark is always on the lookout for runners whose diets consist almost solely of "bagels, bagels, bagels." "I like to look at a person's relationships with food and with exercise," she notes. "How flexible and varied is their diet? Do they allow themselves to eat pizza and ice cream once in a while, or are these considered 'bad' foods? And are they pounding and punishing, just to reach or maintain a certain weight or size, or are they focused on training and setting realistic goals?"

Amenorrhea

Restricting calories and/or certain types of food can cause tremendous physical and hormonal changes that are associated with changes in menstrual status. A deficit between energy intake and energy expenditure is emerging as the most likely underlying cause of amenorrhea in female athletes, notes Barbara Drinkwater, Ph.D. Research consistently shows that amenorrheic runners consume 200 to 900 fewer calories per day than female runners who have regular menstrual cycles. And runners who don't menstruate or who have irregular periods place themselves at a high risk for osteoporosis—a condition characterized by significant and perhaps irreversible bone loss that can result in fractures of the pelvis, hip and spine.

"Amenorrhea is a red flag that the female runner has gone too far in her training," Drinkwater points out. "For most women, it's a signal that estrogen production has dropped to a dangerously low level." She points to the following as red flags: not having a first regular period by age 16 and missing a period for 3 or more consecutive months. "Listen to your body," she advises. "For most women, skipping cycles or failing to menstruate is a signal that estrogen levels have dropped to those of postmenopausal women, placing you at great risk for serious health problems."

Osteoporosis

Osteoporosis is premature bone loss and/or inadequate bone formation that leads to bone deterioration and an increased risk of fracture. This bone loss appears to be tied to low estrogen levels, notes Drinkwater, who has clients in their 20s and 30s whose bones look similar to those of women in their 70s or 80s. And more and more studies are finding that most bone loss in female runners is permanent, she adds, confirming the seriousness of this problem. A few studies show that bone loss can be halted, or reversed to a very limited degree, with a slight weight gain, a resumption of regular periods and the consumption of at least 1,500mg of calcium per day. However, complete replacement of lost bone doesn't seem possible, Drinkwater notes; this is why she stresses the importance of paying attention to your body—and doing so now rather than later.

As for performance, Clark conducted a 5-year study of 89 elite female runners that revealed that the highest numbers of stress fractures occurred among those who were leanest, who focused heavily on diet and weight and who didn't have regular menstrual periods. Asks Clark, "How can you be the best athlete if you're injured?" Other studies document markedly reduced respiratory capacity and decreased speed in female runners who lose weight through dieting, compared with "control" runners who don't diet.

Restricting calories and specific foods deprives the body of much-needed fuel, such as energy to fuel a race or training session, carbohydrates to replace glycogen loss and protein to build and repair tissue. In bowing to pressure to lose weight, Drinkwater points out, female runners don't just lose fat; they also lose muscle. And poor nutrition can result in chronic fatigue, increased susceptibility to infection, poor or delayed healing and recovery from injury, anemia and electrolyte imbalances. Ultimately, all these changes adversely affect performance.

PREGNANCY

Women runners, even the fittest, used to be discouraged from exercising beyond the most rudimentary level during pregnancy. The concern was that fetal growth and the mother's

ARE YOU JEOPARDIZING YOUR PERFORMANCE AND HEALTH?

Use these questions as a guide to assess whether your health and performance are at risk as a result of how you approach eating and training. These questions target athletes who diet and exercise with the goal of reaching a specific, and perhaps unrealistic, weight, rather than training to meet racing goals and eating to satisfy their appetites and nutritional needs. If you answer yes to any of these questions, speak with your doctor or a dietitian/sports nutritionist. To find a sports nutritionist in your area, call the American Dietetic Association at (800) 366–1655.

Are you preoccupied with food, calories, body shape and weight?

Are you afraid of gaining weight or becoming fat, even if you're moderately or very underweight or have a low percentage of body fat?

Over the past year (or longer), have you maintained a lower-than-"normal" body weight by severely restricting caloric intake, i.e., to less than 80 percent of your energy expenditure; severely limiting your food choices or food groups; and/or working out to a much greater degree than runners of a similar ability or than what's required for success at your level of running?

Is your weight loss or maintenance of a very low body weight voluntary and not caused by any illness or other specific condition or disorder?

Have you stopped menstruating, or have your periods become irregular?

Other factors to consider include gastrointestinal complaints; frequent self-induced vomiting or using laxatives or diuretics for at least one month; and bingeing (up to eight times a month for at least 3 months).

weight gain would be decreased by unhealthy amounts. The American College of Obstetrics and Gynecology (ACOG) said that pregnant women should limit strenuous activity to no more than 15 minutes and keep their heart rates below 140 beats per minute. So much for any kind of real running.

But as more women runners ignored this well-meant advice, and as research on pregnancy and exercise advanced, that thinking has changed. Current studies indicate that vigorous exercise, including running, during pregnancy can benefit both the mother and the baby. So in 1994, ACOG changed its recommendations; they're now broader and more permissive, stating that healthy, active women can continue running during pregnancy as long as they keep in close contact with their doctors and use common sense. As with so many other matters in running, we're finding that we can't lay down universal rules, and that the runner's intuition is often the best guide.

It used to be feared that the fetus inside a running mother would be damaged by decreased blood flow and oxygen to the uterus when the mother trains. It's now been shown that compensatory mechanisms exist for this, as well as to ensure that both the mother and her baby have adequate fuel during exercise, particularly in the middle to late stages of pregnancy, when fetal growth takes off. Pregnancy outcomes—including the baby's weight gain during pregnancy and weight at birth; the newborn's head circumference; complications of pregnancy, labor and delivery; type of delivery, i.e., C-section versus vaginal; and the newborn's overall physical condition, which serves as an indicator of subsequent neurological development—also seem to be unaffected by the level and intensity of exercise throughout pregnancy.

Still other studies indicate that women who continue to exercise throughout pregnancy report having far fewer adverse symptoms of pregnancy—such as nausea, heartburn, leg cramps and insomnia—than do women who opt out of regular exercise. And a recent study conducted at Case Western Reserve School of Medicine in Cleveland found that, contrary to popular belief, adequate weight gain—about 30 pounds, compared with the 39 to 42 pounds gained by nonexercisers in the study—is possible for active pregnant women. (ACOG recommends a gain of 25 to 35 pounds during pregnancy for most women.)

How much you run during pregnancy will come down to listening to your body. Joan ran 5 miles on the morning of one of her two deliveries, and she remembers this fondly as one of the peak running experiences of her life. In June 1995, Sue Olsen, while 8½ months pregnant, finished the Grandma's Marathon in Duluth, MN, in 4:00:50. The next week, she competed in a 24-hour race around Minnesota's Lake Harriet. Less than 30 hours later, she gave birth to a healthy son who weighed 7 pounds, 3 ounces.

Of course, these are extremes. Even with ACOG's green light, at some point during even the healthiest of pregnancies and among the most-active mothers-to-be, intensive weight-bearing movement—including running—almost always becomes too uncomfortable to continue. Based on several top runners' experiences, it then becomes a matter of doing what's comfortable. Janis Klecker, the 1992 Olympic Marathon Trials winner and a mother of three (including twins), faced this question. About 6 months into her second pregnancy, Klecker says, she had gotten so big and was running so slowly that it was discouraging. So she traded in her running gear and her 4- to 7-mile days for swimming, aquarunning, walking and riding a stationary bike. Gwyn Coogan, also a 1992 Olympian, continued to run until about the seventh month of her pregnancy, at which point she says her workouts began to feel very different. She started hiking, biking and swimming—activities she enjoys, but for which she usually has little or no time.

New Zealand Olympian Chris Pfitzinger took a slightly different approach. She began tapering off as soon as she found out she was pregnant: she had been covering 8 to 18 miles a day, but she cut back to 5 or 6 in the early stages of her pregnancy. By her eighth month, she says, she was "trotting around barefoot in the grass about one to two miles a day and enjoying every minute of it." And Joan Nesbit, the 1995 national cross country champion, stopped running and began swimming 5½ months into her pregnancy. When running becomes uncomfortable or impossible, she advises, "transfer your passion for running, fitness and the outdoors to other activities." Chances are, she says, you'll come back refreshed and eager to return to running rather than feeling worn out. Klecker agrees, saying that keeping a healthy mental attitude about taking a break allowed her to return to running well. (She ran a 2:39 marathon 10 months after her twins were born.)

Flexibility is also the key to returning successfully to running after pregnancy. A rule of thumb is to wait about 6 weeks after a vaginal delivery (longer after a C-section) to return to working out. It's probably OK to get a jump on your training, but all new mothers need to go slowly, especially during the first few months after delivery. Joan believes that returning to running too quickly after her first delivery may have contributed to her ongoing problem of hip misalignment.

The problem with coming back too quickly, Nesbit points out, is that "you'll never know if you've come back too fast until it's too late." And because your joints and ligaments remain loose for about 9 months to a year after delivery, you're especially prone to injury during that time. Avoid hills and rough terrain and trails, she advises, and in general, start out by erring on the side of caution.

The pace at which you resume training will vary considerably, depending on your experiences during pregnancy and during and immediately after delivery. Klecker found that her return to running, especially after her twins were born, was "an exercise in patience." She started from scratch about 8 weeks after delivery, with 9-minute miles of walking and jogging. She worked her way up to 5 miles a day at an 8-minute pace, and in her first race, 8 months after her twins were born, she ran a 26:56 8K, less than a minute off her PR. Coogan jumped right back into training—just 10 days after Katrina was born in November 1993. Within 12 weeks, Coogan had placed sixth at the U.S. trials for the world cross country championships.

Remember that these are very goal-oriented women, for whom racing is one of the most important parts of life. Even the ones who have returned quickly to top running concede that they may have rushed things, and advise that the more gradual your return to your pre-pregnancy program, the more successful you're likely to be, both as a runner and a mother.

BIRTH CONTROL

At least two studies have found that women runners are less likely than their sedentary counterparts to take oral contraceptives. The pill does slightly reduce aerobic capacity, so it makes sense that competitive women would shy away from it. Many women runners also report that they just find it harder to feel as "sharp" as they would like while taking the pill. The best blanket advice is to experiment to see what works for you. If other methods work for you besides the pill, use them. Most women runners who have found a successful alternative to the pill prefer to avoid oral contraceptives.

RUNNING BRAS AND OTHER APPAREL

As I've said elsewhere, fit is the most important feature to seek in running apparel. For women, this means that the best apparel will be more than just smaller versions of men's gear.

Women's needs, after all, are different. Shorts need to be wider at the hips and longer from waist to crotch. Tops need smaller armholes. Most manufacturers now make running apparel that takes these factors into consideration, and there are many companies that devote their entire lines to meeting the needs of active women.

The one piece of apparel every woman runner should invest in is a good running bra. Although no evidence shows that running braless damages breasts, most women, regardless of their breast size, feel more comfortable wearing a bra when they run. Even though there's a line of running apparel with my name on it, I'm not going to presume to know the ins and outs of choosing a running bra. Here's what Joan recommends:

- No clasps. Find a bra that slips over your head; front and back clasps can dig into your skin.
- No exposed seams inside. These can cause painful chafing.
- ½ to ¾-inch shoulder straps. Thin straps can dig into your shoulders.
- A wide elastic chest band to prevent the bra from riding up.
- Appropriate fabrics. Try cotton/spandex blends, with some polyester for durability. If you need more support, look for a bra that has Lycra.
- Get the size you usually wear, or one as close to it as possible. A bra is too small if you can't fit your thumb under the shoulder straps and the elastic chest band. Conversely, a bra is too loose if its straps slip off your shoulders.
- Always try on a bra before you buy it. In the dressing room, run in place, do jumping jacks, touch your toes and swing your arms around.

Getting Older

MAKING AGING A POSITIVE

You can beat aging, rather than it beating you.
Changing your goals doesn't mean that you've given in.
If you dictate the standards of your success,
then you're in control.

As I approach age 50, I'm happy that I still have a full head of hair. Not having been through it, I can only conjecture about what going bald is like, but I think it would be similar to how I think about my running as I age. The changes are subtle, almost imperceptible from day to day, and even in retrospect it's difficult to point to a certain period and say with confidence, "That's when it really started." But a look in the mirror—or at the stopwatch—says it all. You're undeniably different, and what you used to take for granted is now the stuff of your dreams.

But like baldness, aging's effect on your running is nothing to be ashamed of. In fact, it can be a chance to learn more about what really matters as you adjust to the changed reality. In this chapter, we'll look at how to deal with the inevitable slowing and other changes that come to your running as you age. As I keep emphasizing, the fundamental factor in running for a lifetime is finding what works for you and what you find enjoyable. In the context of this chapter, remember that changing your goals doesn't mean that you've given in. If you dictate the standards of your success, then you're in control. You beat aging, rather than it beating you.

MY, HOW I'VE AGED

Don't get me wrong. When I think about how my running feels in my late 40s compared to my late 20s, I don't exactly go skipping down the street, and not just because to do so would probably injure me. I get more fatigued today running 70 to 90 miles a week than I used to get when I averaged 130 miles a week. Mileage aside, I just feel, well, older. I still have the energy to do the things that I want, but I'm more aware of being tired when doing them. And when I get up in the morning, it takes me awhile to get going. On days when I'm not pressed for time, I sometimes putter around the house for an hour or so before heading out for a run. I used to be able to start a run immediately, anytime, anywhere. Now, I need to walk around a bit, loosen up and make a more conscious effort to get myself out the door.

There have been other changes as I've aged. Starting in my late 30s and early 40s, I noticed a pretty much perpetual soreness in my legs that wasn't there before. I would definitely get sore 20 years ago, but when I did, it was an acute soreness, limited to one spot on my legs, and I could usually figure out why I had it. For example, if I wore spikes on the track, I could usually count on my calves being sore the next day, and I could count on that soreness disappearing within a few days. What I experience now is different. It's more low-grade, but it's almost always there.

I've noticed some psychological changes, too. Speed work is harder than it used to be. I don't mean in terms of the times that I run; obviously, they're slower than when I was among the best marathoners in the world. And I don't even mean that speed work is harder in terms of, for example, how painful a 400-meter repeat feels. I mean that mentally, it's harder to get myself to push to the point that I know I should. This is especially so on longer intervals, such as mile repeats. I used to be very good at attacking these in workouts. When I would run with my Greater Boston Track Club teammates, I would pride myself on being right up there on these longer intervals, because I knew that when we did the shorter stuff, like 400-meter repeats, that I wouldn't be able to keep up with them. So it's strange now to find that I can still nail a session of 400-meter repeats pretty well, but mile intervals are harder to face.

I think part of that is because I do most of my training

JETS

alone these days. This is something that many masters runners face. If you ran in college, for example, you were used to having a group to run with. This is especially helpful on the harder stuff like track workouts. I was able to continue that structure for a long time; I knew that it helped improve the quality of my speed work and, therefore, my races. I really liked the feeling of a bunch of us being out there together on the track helping each other out. When I was dragging a bit, I knew that the others would help to pull me along to a better workout than I would have done on my own. Now that I do nearly all of my hard running alone, it's harder to feel as if I finish the workouts as pleasantly drained as I used to. And I know it takes more concentration to get through them on my own. While this can be good, because it teaches you to rely on yourself more, as you must in races, I think almost all runners who have trained with a group and by themselves will tell you that it's easier to get in a high-quality speed session with others.

One of the first-noticed and universal changes that runners note with age is a decreased ability to recover from hard efforts. When I was training hard for the marathon, most of my running was at a moderately hard pace. I just wanted to get in the miles. Except on days when I was doing a track workout in the afternoon, I would do my main run of the day in the morning, usually at a good clip. My second run of the day was usually shorter, but it would be at about the same pace as the morning run. If I tried that now, I'd be dragging. If I do a second run for the day, it's seldom more than 5 miles long, and it's noticeably slower than my longer run in the morning. It's a true recovery run.

Now that I've completely depressed you, let's put all of this in perspective. To prosper in your running over a long time, you have to be able to look at things from a different perspective. Let's take the example of my slower afternoon run. Yes, I could sit around and bemoan my diminished capacities, but what good would that do? So I can't run 130 miles a week at 6:00 per mile anymore? Well, I couldn't when I was 20, either, and it didn't bother me then. Also, many of my evening runs are with a friend and neighbor, Joe Martino. I usually run a bit slower with Joe than on my own. There's nothing wrong with that. If Joe and I run 5 miles together, he's getting in a good training effort, and I'm getting in some more miles at a relaxed enough pace that they're not going to break me down. More important, I really look forward to these runs, because I love the thought of the two of us being out there spending the time talking about anything and everything and helping each other reach our goals.

Frank Hutchinson: Reborn with Age

Competition calls some people at an early age. Phenoms like Jim Ryun and Gerry Lindgren were already star runners while still in high school. For Frank Hutchinson, of Los Osos, California, the running bug didn't bite until later in life. But after a whiff of success in a few road races, he answered competition's call with gusto, finding a richer life in the sport and in always trying to improve his performances.

He first started running consistently in 1977 at age 25, while taking a physical conditioning class in college. "I was gaining a lot of weight then," he says. "I went from 170 to about 190 pounds. I knew my lifestyle wasn't going to change that much, so running seemed like a great way to control my weight without giving up everything else."

Frank did more than stay trim. Although his original intent wasn't to compete, he started entering local road races and was able to win a few of them. "I was never at the higher levels like Mark [Conover, an occasional training partner who won the 1988 Olympic Marathon Trials], but I had some success in the smaller races," Frank says. Those performances have been kindling for a competitive fire that still burns hot.

"I feel like my best performances may still be in front of me," he claims. "I ran my PR in the mile [4:29] just before I turned forty." That was in 1992. Now in the masters ranks, he has an opportunity to let his running carry him a long way. "The St. George Marathon in Utah gives a trip to Japan to the first master in that race," he explains. "I got fourth in my first try and second overall the next year. I'd like to try and stay competitive on every level, but the age group change gives me new incentive."

As he moves through his mid-40s, Frank doesn't believe that he's conceded much by aging a few years. "I just need to keep the intensity up," he says. "I need to push myself and I can still improve." His job as a dialysis unit technician forces him to keep irregular hours and makes finding the time to train difficult, but he manages. "Sometimes when I get home from work the last thing I feel like doing is running," he admits. "I can't train the way I used to. Before St. George, I would do a long, hard day, then take a day off. It was unorthodox, but I think it prepared me well."

Injuries have also slowed him somewhat. Sore knees and plantar fasciitis have inhibited his performances over the last year, changing his plans slightly. He doesn't train as tenaciously as he used to, but now he believes that he's smarter. "You see a lot of people who trained very hard all through high school and college. They get burned out," he says. "I would've liked to have run in high school, but it's okay that I didn't. I know I'm not going to burn out." Frank says he will continue to run as long as he is physically able.

Competitiveness is a factor that keeps his legs churning, but it isn't the only thing. His original motivation of running for fitness still gets him out the door. Just the feeling of a good run is reward enough. "It's almost like a high when you're in the middle of a good run," he says. With most races splitting results into age categories, creatures of competition like Frank can stay in the hunt for years to come.

THE COMPONENTS OF FITNESS AND HOW THEY CHANGE WITH AGE

To understand better what happens to your fitness as you get older, let's look at some of the main components of fitness. After a brief description of each, you'll see two more blocks of text: how that component changes with age, and what you as a runner can do to influence the rate and degree of change. I'll say more about this later, but keep in mind that these components of fitness all play off one another. That is, as something like your body composition changes, this affects your muscular strength; in turn, a change in muscular strength can affect how much you can train, and this can affect your aerobic capacity. My point is to view your fitness holistically, and understand that we age systemically, not body part by body part. I like looking at some of the changes that occur separately, though, because I think that it gives you a better idea of all that's going on inside you.

Aerobic Capacity

WHAT IT IS: To work, your muscles produce a compound, adenosine triphosphate (ATP), that they can obtain three ways. First, from ATP stored in the muscle. Second, by breaking down muscle glycogen (your muscles' main fuel) without oxygen. These two methods are anaerobic ("without oxygen") production of energy. We'll look at those in a moment. For now, let's consider the third source of ATP, energy derived from breaking down carbohydrates, fats and, in extreme circumstances, protein using oxygen. This is aerobic energy production. How efficiently you do this—that is, use the oxygen that you breathe in—is your aerobic capacity. Your VO_2 max is a measurement of your aerobic capacity; specifically, it is the maximal volume of oxygen, measured in milliliters, that you can use per kilogram of bodyweight in one minute. Although there are many things that determine success in distance running, most exercise scientists agree that your VO_2 max is the single best indicator of your endurance potential. For reference, David Costill, Ph.D., who is one of the seminal figures in running research in this country, once tested my VO_2 max. It was 78 (milliliters per kilogram per minute). Dr. Costill told me that the average 20-year-old male has a VO_2 max of from 44 to 47. Mine was so high partly because of my genetics, but also because of my training. As with all other physical characteristics, there's great variance among people's VO_2 max. No matter how hard you train, yours isn't going to go beyond a genetically predetermined level. It takes massive amounts of training to reach that—remember, I averaged 130 miles per week for several years—but with a moderate amount of training, you can bump it up pretty good. Dr. Costill told me that the opposite also happens. In the 1960s, he tested a 2:17 marathoner whose VO_2 max was 72.4. He tested him again 3 years later, during which the one-time 2:17 guy hadn't run a step. His VO_2 max had dropped to 47.6, a decrease of roughly one third. I mention this to illustrate how much you can do to boost or, at least maintain, your VO_2 max. It just goes to show you what consistent exercise (or the lack thereof) at any level can do.

WHAT HAPPENS WITH AGE: Put bluntly, your VO_2 max drops. Past age 30, it declines by about 1 percent per year. This decrease can be slowed with regular aerobic training, but it's unavoidable.

WHAT YOU CAN DO WITH AGE: Fight the good fight. As I said, everyone's aerobic capacity declines with age, but there are three important things to keep in mind. First, as a runner you're declining from a much higher starting point than your sedentary peers. I haven't had my VO_2 max tested recently, but it's obviously still quite high, thanks to my consistent training over the years. It's still well above that of the average 20-year-old. To me, that's exciting. Second, although some decline is inevitable, not enough research has been done to distinguish how much of the decline that's observed in long-term runners is because of age, and how much is due to training differently. To use myself as an example, it's no surprise that my VO_2 max in my late 40s isn't what it was in my late 20s. Part of that is the aging process, but how much? These days, I run 70 to 90 miles per week. Twenty years ago, it was more like 130 miles per week. If I could still handle that much training, I'm willing to bet that my aerobic capacity wouldn't have declined as much. This ties into the third point to keep in mind. If you're a long-term runner, you can probably better duplicate the training of your heyday, at least in terms of volume, than I can. I put up a pretty tough standard to maintain. But if you ran 40 miles a week 15 years ago and have stayed relatively injury-free, you can probably come close to running that mileage now, so although your aerobic capacity will decrease, it might not be by as great a percentage as mine. And if you started running past the age of 35 or so, your aerobic capacity is going to increase for the first several years of your running career, regardless of aging. The bottom line to aerobic capacity and aging: the more aerobic exercise you get, the longer it will take to decline.

Anaerobic Capacity

WHAT IT IS: This is your body's ability to produce energy without using oxygen. As I said above, there are two ways for it to do this. One is by using the ATP that exists within your muscle cells. For distance runners, this isn't something we really care about, because this form of energy is designed to be used immediately in one explosive action that lasts for 3 to 5 seconds. An example is when you give a heavy box one big shove to the top shelf of a closet. In the sports world, think of a shotputter just as he heaves the shot, or a sprinter in the instant that she explodes out of the starting blocks. The second source of anaerobic energy is when glycogen is converted to ATP without oxygen; your muscles can sustain this for only 20 to 60 seconds. When you sprint 100 meters, this is an anaerobic effort. It's over before it really hurts—no wonder I've always been jealous of sprinters!—but if you maintained that effort much longer, such as in a 200-meter sprint, your muscles will start to burn, and you'll have to work very hard to maintain your form and speed. And if you've ever tried to sprint for 400 meters, or one lap of the track, you certainly know what happens when you try to sustain anaerobic exercise for too long. In runner's lingo, you start to tie up, or lose form and slow drastically. This second type of anaerobic capacity is worth working on if you're going to be racing, especially at shorter distances. It's what allows you to kick in those last few hundred yards of a 10K. Being able to do so well can take at least a few seconds off your time, not to mention being able to catch and pass other runners.

WHAT HAPPENS WITH AGE: Your fast-twitch fibers are the ones that you use when you run anaerobically. All muscle fibers degenerate with age. Fast-twitch ones do so the quickest.

WHAT YOU CAN DO WITH AGE: You've really got to work to maintain your anaerobic capacity. This is kind of a simplification, but some research indicates that if fast-twitch fibers aren't used regularly with age, their ability to fire is lost permanently. In other words, they go into early retirement, and

EARLY RETIREMENT

A few years ago I retired from the marathon. My reasons were many. I was still trying to do around 25 races a year; the business side of my life was becoming more complex; I was traveling more; I wanted to spend more time with my two daughters—all of these factors made it harder for me to feel like I was training effectively for the marathon. I wanted to be competitive in them, not just run them for the heck of it. But doing the training I thought was necessary to remain competitive kept breaking me down; I couldn't make it to the starting line!

Also, once I was in my 40s, the incentives were removed more and more. In 1990, I was the fifth master at the Boston Marathon at age 42 in 2:20:46, a time that would have won every Boston until the early 1960s. I was proud of what I had accomplished, but there's also something in my psyche that really enjoys being acknowledged by others, and it was as if my finish wasn't good enough. People acted like I had let them down! As much as I knew that with masters running more than any other type, personal satisfaction has to be your main motivation, I started thinking about retiring from the marathon.

It's turned out that this has been a smart way to train. Maybe Johnny Kelley, who won the Boston Marathon twice and has run it more times than anyone else, is the only person on the planet who has succeeded at the marathon for a lifetime. The marathon is a great challenge and a super thrill, but it's good to have different races be your focus at different times of your life. This keeps your running more interesting and gives you new ways of maintaining motivation.

no amount of coaxing will bring them out. Regular speed work will keep them active. Because not everyone wants to do speed work, and because I don't think you should do it year-round if you decide to do speed work, I recommend that all runners past the age of 40 who want to maintain a good deal of their anaerobic capacity do striders. These are controlled, fast runs of 20 seconds or so at a pace that you think you could maintain for half a mile to a mile. These are good to do at the end of an easy run, when you're nice and warmed up. They're very convenient—all you need is a flat stretch that's about 100 meters long. When you run these, you want to concentrate on good form and on staying relaxed. Rest for 30 to 60 seconds between; you don't want these to turn into grueling workouts. They're short enough that they shouldn't take too much out of you, but wait to start the next one until your breathing is under control and you know that you can run it fast but under control, rather than straining, as you might toward the end of a 400-meter repeat. Do 10 to 12 in a session. These have many benefits, illustrating how the components of fitness relate to each other. When you run striders, you move through a greater range of motion than on your steady distance runs. This is an active way to maintain flexibility. Also, the faster running that you do on these demands more powerful contractions from your leg muscles, and thereby also helps to preserve muscle strength.

Body Composition

WHAT IT IS: All of the parts that make up your total body weight can be split into two groups: lean body mass and body fat. Body composition is usually stated in terms of your body fat percentage, or the percentage of your weight that is body fat. This is a much better measure of how healthful your body make-up is than weight. We tend to assume that all skinny people have a low percentage of body fat, while all heavy people have a high percentage of body fat. This is wrong, and it's why I'm not a big fan of the charts that show desirable weights for heights. You can smoke and drink a lot and not exercise and be skinny, but your body fat percentage is going to be pretty high, because you don't do anything that develops your muscles. In contrast, body builders are usually above average in weight, but they can have body fat percentages that are as low as those of distance runners. There are several ways to measure body composition, such as skin-fold calipers and underwater weighing, but if you're honest with yourself, you can fairly say whether you have too much body fat. One way to tell over time is how your clothes fit. As we'll see in a minute, your weight can stay the same while your body fat increases. If your weight is unchanged but your clothes are tighter, especially in the places where you tend to store fat, your body composition has most likely changed.

WHAT HAPPENS WITH AGE: You can probably guess this one. With age, your metabolism slows, so even if you eat the same amount and are just as active as you were 20 years ago, you'll probably store some extra fat. Also, we lose lean body mass with age. The old saw about muscle turning into fat isn't true—biochemically speaking, they're different materials—but it sure can seem that way when your well-defined biceps start getting flabby. It's the double whammy of tending to store more fat while simultaneously losing lean body mass that can make this such a frustrating effort. If you're a long-time runner, add to that the likelihood that you've cut back on your mileage since your prime, and you can see why this is such a frustrating issue for so many people.

WHAT YOU CAN DO WITH AGE: Lift weights. The more you do to build muscle, the more you can keep the encroachment of increased body fat at bay. Remember that body composition has to do with percentages. Even if you don't store extra body fat, your body fat *percentage* will still increase because of losing lean body mass. In 1991, two-time Olympic medalist Frank Shorter underwent a series of physiological tests to see how he compared at age 43 to his peak in 1975, at age 27.

His weight hadn't changed, but his body fat had doubled. (Of course, we're talking about Frank Shorter here, so even a doubling didn't exactly mean that he was bursting out of his shirts.) Also, if you look at two people who are the same weight but of different body fat percentages, the one with the lower percentage probably burns more calories, all other things being equal. That's because muscles require more energy to maintain themselves than do fat.

Muscular Strength

WHAT IT IS: This is the amount of force that your muscles can exert when they contract or extend. It's usually measured in terms of a one-repetition maximum, such as how much you can bench press.

WHAT HAPPENS WITH AGE: As we've seen, muscle strength decreases if you don't do anything about it. That's because you lose lean body mass as you age; obviously, less muscle means less muscular strength. Also, as mentioned in the anaerobic capacity section, your fast-twitch muscle fibers often degenerate at a quicker rate than do your slow-twitch fibers, accelerating the loss of strength, especially if, like many people as they age, you avoid strength-building activities in favor of endurance exercise.

WHAT YOU CAN DO WITH AGE: Same as for body composition—use it or lose it. Devise a strength training program that works all of the major muscle groups through a good range of motion. Note that this doesn't have to mean hitting the Universal machine at the local health club twice a week, although that's certainly a good option. Striders, speed work and uphill running require your legs to work hard enough to count as muscle-maintaining activities. Pushups, chinups and dips can do much for your upper body. Find a strength training program that you can honestly say that you'll stick with. Consistency is key here.

Flexibility

WHAT IT IS: This is your ability to move your body through a desirable range of motion. There isn't a universal standard, such as, "Your hamstrings should be flexible enough so you can bend over and put your palms on the floor while keeping your legs straight." Rather, for distance runners, it's a subjective measure of how easily your body can attain the suppleness that's necessary to accommodate the range of motion without tearing or straining that your training and racing requires. You want to be able to run your 400-meter repeats, for example, without feeling constrained by tightness in your hips and hamstrings. You also want to be able to do your normal range of training and racing paces without getting sore every time you try to push your limits a bit. Good flexibility allows your muscles, tendons and ligaments to stretch occasionally a little beyond their normal range of motion without you getting tight, sore or injured in the process.

WHAT HAPPENS WITH AGE: Generally, flexibility decreases. (By this point, are you surprised by that?) As with aerobic capacity, though, it can be difficult to determine how much is inevitable and how much is due to your habits. Your muscles lose some resiliency with age, so even the most conscientious ballerina isn't going to be as limber at age 55 as she was at age 25. But most of our lack of flexibility with age is brought on by lifestyle. There are a number of examples. If, as you've aged, you've emphasized more easy running, then you're not moving through as full a range of motion as you used to, and your flexibility will suffer. Also, many readers of this book are going to have deskbound jobs. Sitting in pretty much the same position for long periods of time leaves you tight, and all the more so after 10 or 20 or 30 years of doing so. And let's be honest: some of us get more lax about the supplementary parts of our program as we age, and that includes regular post-run stretching.

WHAT YOU CAN DO WITH AGE: Are the answers becoming pretty obvious to you by now? First, maintain (or start!) your stretching program. Pay special attention to those areas that trouble you the most. Try to get in at least four post-run stretching sessions of 10 to 15 minutes each per week. Run a variety of paces in your training so that you're not always moving through the same range of motion. If you have a sedentary job, try to get up and move about at least once an hour. Distance runners who have sedentary jobs need to be especially mindful of keeping their hamstrings loose.

Ruth Grimes: Shifting Gears

Sometimes, only through a loss can you find a big gain. When Ruth Grimes was going through a divorce in 1981, a friend suggested that she try running to take her mind off things. In her first attempt, dressed in jeans and tennis shoes, she could only make it a few blocks.

"I really don't know why I kept trying," she says. "I guess I'm just stubborn." Whatever it was, Ruth found a new companion in running. Soon she was able to cover the distance more easily, and placed first in her age group in the first 5K she ever ran. She was hooked. By the next year, she had run her first marathon and was racing all the time. Upon entering the masters bracket in 1989, she was ready to chalk up more wins. "I was on a hardware hunt, I guess," she says.

Perhaps she was a little overzealous with her new love. Injuries followed injuries, dampening her progress, but not her enthusiasm. Despite five stress fractures, Ruth still sees running as one of the most positive forces influencing her today. "It's totally changed my life," she claims. "I met my husband through running. My son's a runner and studying to be a podiatrist. I've met so many people, but the biggest thing it's given me is self-confidence. I used to be quiet and shy. If I couldn't sit in the back of a room during a meeting, I didn't want to be there."

Her newfound faith in herself has allowed her to excel on the job as well. She works in Berkeley, California, as a planner for the local fire department. "When I know I can run fifty miles, giving a speech in front of the City Council is nothing," she says. Her job has been very supportive of her athletic endeavors. "I run during my lunch hour. The fire department is very happy to encourage better health in its employees."

One of her biggest thrills in running came about because of her job when she represented the City of Berkeley at a marathon in Japan. "I got the real elite athlete treatment there," she recalls, "meeting the emperor's son, hearing my name at the start. I got to meet Allison Roe, who was a hero of mine when I started running."

Ruth ran her marathon PR in 1986, a 3:27 effort that won the Modesto Marathon. Now, she's content to enter fewer races as long as she's able to continue running. "When I turned forty, I went a little crazy with the racing. I think that's what got me hurt. I only enter a couple of races a year, but it's just as gratifying for me to just put in the miles now. There's nothing better than going for a long run in the hills. It helps you clear your mind. It puts your life back in order. If I can go for a couple hours on the trails, by myself, I come back refreshed, not tired."

Running has given Ruth a balance in her life. She and her husband were copresidents of a San Francisco-area running club for a few years. "Everyone in Berkeley knows me as the woman who runs all the time. Even the mayor," she laughs. Her only regret is the injuries. "I wish I would've taken it easy. I should've given my body more time to recover."

Whether she's racing, staying in shape or just clearing her mind, Ruth will always run. "I fully intend to keep running for the duration of my life, no matter what."

Bone Density

WHAT IT IS: This is a measure of how much stress your bones can tolerate. Runners need good bone density so that the pounding of training doesn't lead to stress fractures.

WHAT HAPPENS WITH AGE: Bones shrink with age, meaning that a smaller unit has to take the same amount of pounding. More important, bones start becoming thinner after about the age of 30. Women lose bone density at a greater rate than men, especially once they're past menopause.

WHAT YOU CAN DO WITH AGE: This is one area in which your regular steady runs will bring most of the benefits that are to be had. Weight bearing exercise such as running strengthens bones. So does weight training. Older women runners should also be especially mindful of their calcium intake. See the chart "Dairy's Queen" in the diet section of Chapter 2 for the best dietary sources.

THE MASTERS INTERCONNECTION

Just as the physiological changes that occur with age affect your running, so too do changes in your lifestyle. I don't have as clear cut a set of answers about this matter as I do about, say, combating the loss of muscle mass that starts in your 30s, but I do want to call attention to the matter so that

you're aware of it and, if need be, can devise ways to make it a positive.

I'll use myself as an example. In the past few years, the promotional side of my various business involvements has increased. I simply work more hours than I used to, often based on someone else's schedule, and many times requiring me to travel. Naturally, this leaves me more tired. This can lead to me cutting back either the length or intensity, or both, of my training. Or, I might plow ahead with the same level of effort, but because I've gone into it more tired, it takes more out of me. Neither of these developments are particularly good for the big picture. In the first case, fewer distance runs or less speed work means that I won't be as sharp as I might be in my next few races. In the second case, in which I stick with my original workouts despite my increased fatigue, I'm more likely to get sore or injured from the training. This might make me alter my running form a little, and set off a chain reaction of compensations, and the whole process can snowball.

I think about how interconnected all the parts of my training are, and how much trickier it gets to strike the right balance, when I reflect on my case of plantar fasciitis. I believe that I got the injury by changing my running in response to getting older. In my 20s and 30s, I ran some of my runs on the grass or dirt on the side of the road, rather than always on the asphalt or concrete of the road or sidewalk. This helped my calves and tendons and ligaments in my feet and legs to stay looser. As I hit 40, and thought that I needed better traction and surer footing, I stopped doing this, and switched to hard surfaces only. It turned out that this change of surface made me tighter in my calves and Achilles tendons at the very time that my connective tissue was starting to lose its elasticity. Those two together were too much for my plantar fascia, and they remained bothersome for a year and a half.

This was an eye opener. I've always been aware of how the other parts of my life influence my running, but now I realize that with age I have to consider almost everything I do. I don't have any hard and fast rules about how to apply this discovery to your situation, and I certainly don't want to encourage runners to overanalyze their training, because then much of the fun is gone. But as you become an older runner, you need to pay attention to matters you used to be able to get away with ignoring.

MOTIVATION FOR MASTERS

When you become a masters runner, and especially when you get in to your 50s, 60s, and beyond, maintaining motivation can be tough. As you get older, you find fewer of your age-group peers out there, and at some point, you'll notice that no matter what you do, your times are getting slower. I find that my motivation in races is getting more difficult as I age. I don't seem to be as comfortable or relaxed in my races as I used to be; they all seem like hard work. It's also increasingly difficult to get a sense of my training being easy; I always seem to be a little more tired than I'd like. I know some of that is because I'm pushing limits and on the verge of setting records, so it's to be expected, but I've still had to make some mental adjustments as I've gotten older.

When I finally accepted that my age was catching up with me, and that I wasn't going to run 2:11 for the marathon anymore, I thought back to how I felt about running when I started. For me, the basic approach to racing hasn't changed since I was 15. Here, I rely on the clichés. They might be trite, but they're true: I'm always trying to do the best I can. If I'm doing that, what more can I ask of myself? When I was 16 I didn't beat everyone in the world, and now, more than 30 years later, I no longer do, either. I know that I'm not racing against all of the runners in front of me. Although I try to beat as many runners in any race as I can, my true competition is against the people in my age group.

Carl Llewellyn: Not Going Gently into That Good Night

Physicists believe that a body in motion tends to stay in motion, while a body at rest stays at rest unless acted on by an outside force. Carl Llewellyn, of Hagerstown, Maryland, is using this law of momentum to keep himself active as a runner.

Carl has been running steadily since 1966, when, at age 51, he took up the sport for its health benefits. "Once you stop, it's really hard to get going again," he says. "I've never been away from running for more than a month." It's this consistency that allowed him to complete the JFK 50 Mile Run, held on trails and roads in his hometown, at age 80 in November 1995. Carl continues to train and race in a manner that would make most people half his age green with envy.

Good health has helped propel him to longevity. "I'm not a person who gets real sick," he says. "As I get older and visit with friends my age, I realize how lucky I am. Not only because I am still physically able to run, but because my way of thinking is healthier, too. I don't worry about getting varicose veins or arthritis like most other people—I think about my next run. It is something that I enjoy, but I also need to keep it up for good health. You can get a lot of exercise in a short amount of time with running."

Competition is another force that keeps him going. Although he says he dislikes most of the attention that he gets in local papers, he relishes the chance to get out and mix it up on the roads. "There's a guy who's eighty-three or eighty-four who can just about beat me at anything," Carl notes. "I have to work hard to stay ahead of him." He also credits age-group running with allowing him to strive for new goals.

Perhaps the biggest factor pushing Carl is the grassroots support of fellow runners. He says that his friend William "Buzz" Sawyer was "a pioneering spirit of coaching" for him in his early days. A former world-class runner, Sawyer founded the Cumberland Valley Athletic Club and the JFK 50-miler, and encouraged many others to run as a means to better their lives. "Spark plugs like Buzz," he says "can really help big numbers of people." Carl still belongs to several area running clubs. "To take part in the clubs as a volunteer is a good way to give something back to the other runners."

Running has been a big part of his life since he started. "My wife says, 'You always get your run in,'" he admits. "Sometimes I wish I devoted more time to my family like a lot of others who are my age, but running has changed my life so much."

Carl will keep on running as long as he can. And even after he stops, he may have helped many others to get their bodies in motion. "I've made a lot of friends through the sport," he says. "I hope I can help others in the way that I've been helped."

Besides deciding if you did the best you could on a given day, you have to keep adjusting your standards of assessment as you become an older runner. Since I turned 45, the leading women at some major races kept finishing closer and closer behind me. I had never been beaten by a woman, and prolonging that inevitable occurrence as long as possible became a big motivation. It's not that I'm sexist and think women are inferior runners to men, or that I thought I should be ashamed to be beaten by a woman. Rather, I knew that our times were similar, so I made staying ahead of them one of my goals, just as I do for men in my age group who I know will be a threat. With weather and terrain having such an effect on times, this was just one more way for me to evaluate my effort on a given day. It's similar to being in the 50–54 age group, and having a goal that nobody in the 45–49 age group will beat you. In October 1995, at a half marathon, I lost to a woman, Lieve Slegers of Belgium, for the first time. I recognized that it happened, didn't let it get me down and started thinking about other ways for me to assess my performances. That and knowing that you're doing the best you can for your age and current situation are what masters running is all about.

For example, during the summer of 1995, I ran 15:17 for a 5K road race. Afterward, I could have sat around and thought, "Boy, that's depressing—I used to be able to run several of those in a row." That's just self-defeating, though. Instead, I was very happy with the race, because I knew it was the best effort I could have put forth on that night, and it was just seconds off of my American age-group record for the distance. Even so, a worker at the race seemed to take pity on me, because she thought I would be upset about getting second overall. I pointed out that the winner was 27, or 20 years younger than me, but she had no concept of that being significant.

That's part of the way it is when you're a masters runner. Most people have a poor enough understanding of what running performances are worth at any age, and they have even less of a sense of what, for example, a 15:17 5K at age 47 means. You have to get nearly all of your motivation from within, and you have to be adaptable.

What's a good approach when you're setting new goals? First, understand that if you're a long-time runner, you're going to have to train differently than when you were 25. John Walker, who was the first person to break 3:50 for the mile, tried to become the first master to break 4:00 for the distance. He wound up getting continually injured because he tried to train as he had when he first broke 4:00 20 years earlier. When Eammon Coghlan finally became the first master to break 4:00, he did it by recognizing that his approach would have change from when he was at his peak, such as including more easy days between hard efforts, getting more frequent massages, paying more attention to outside stresses in his life, etc. Recognize that no matter how hard or well you train, your physical capabilities deteriorate every 5 years or so.

That's why I like evaluating my performances in 5-year brackets, and why I think races that only have 10-year age brackets do older runners a disservice. I know I sure feel a lot different than I did 5 years ago! But by comparing your efforts to those of your recent past, you can maintain a sense of excitement about your racing. It's just you, the stopwatch and a measured distance. You can't BS that, you can't hype that, and you can't water it down with meaningless scoring as you can in team sports. It's human performance at its purest level. That's why so many people take solace in running, despite it being a hard and tricky sport.

Finally, this is an exciting time to be a masters runner. People are smashing age group records nearly every week, and all of the old thoughts about what our limits are are being rethought. Men in their 70s are trying to break 3 hours for the marathon! Masters running might be a smaller world than the open ranks, but if you have the right attitude, it can still be an intoxicating one.

Getting the Balance Right

WEAVING RUNNING INTO THE FABRIC OF YOUR LIFE

When to run is going to come down to when works best for you on a regular basis. Make it easiest for fitting it in with everything else you have to do.

The easiest way to run for a lifetime is to make it an integral part of your life. If running becomes such a regular part of your life that on most days you're 10 minutes into it before you even realize what's going on, then you've hit on a routine that works for you, and that will go a long way toward ensuring consistency and enjoyment in your running. In this chapter, we'll look at several facets of how to keep running logistically and inspirationally feasible, so it can keep the high priority it should have in your busy life.

FITTING IT IN

By both design and good fortune, I haven't had what you might call a "regular job" for the past 20 years. Some people, then, think that although I have worthwhile ideas on how to train to race, avoid injury, and so on, that I can't speak to their situation as they try to juggle running with a career, a commute, a family and other responsibilities. In many ways, these people are wrong. I'm a father of two young daughters, I own a running store that, on a good day, is a 40-minute drive from my house, I'm involved in an ever-increasing number of business and promotional activities, and I travel more weeks than not during the year. So although my life may not be exactly the same as that of someone who works standard office hours, Monday through Friday, I still think I'm qualified to talk about how to make running a positive, doable force in conjunction with the other facets of your life.

For busy adults, the main problem is always going to be finding the time. In Chapter 1, we looked at how one of the most common excuses that people use for not exercising is lack of time. I don't mean to belittle these concerns, but if it's important to you, you'll find the time. If you're reading this part of the book, it's likely that you recognize running is, and should be, important to you. More often than not, then, the crucial question for you isn't, "Am I going to run today?" but, "When am I going to run today?"

FITTING RUNNING INTO LIFE AND PARENTHOOD

Some of you reading this book might be thinking, "Sure, this is all easy for Bill Rodgers. Running is his job. What about us runners with full-time jobs?" One valuable lesson that I've learned from my wife, Gail, is that what you lack in talent and speed, you can, for the most part, make up for with desire. She has demonstrated this over the years, fitting in running and fitness with being a parent. With a little self-help, motivation, organization and creativity, Gail maintains a decent program while not letting the other parts of her life slip.

Gail views each of her workouts as a personal necessity, rather than something to be squeezed in after everyone else's needs have been met. Having a scheduled workout time, at least 4 or 5 times a week, ensures a much better success rate than hoping to have some free time here or there to train. Of course, this is often easier said than done, especially for parents of babies or very small children, who couldn't care less about your training. Unless you have full-time child care, a supportive spouse with free time to watch the kids or kids who never get sick, you'll have to find ways to deal with the various crises that arise as you try to juggle your needs with your children's.

My first advice to new parents, especially mothers, is to take it easy on yourself, both psychologically and physically. Your fitness schedule *will* get derailed. Many times, in fact. The trick is to do your best each day and to try to stay focused toward your goals, regardless of the circumstances. You don't cancel your vacation because of a flat tire; in the same way, don't give up on achieving your goals because of occasional setbacks.

Second, set realistic goals, but do set them. Without some clear-cut ends in mind, runs can turn into aimless wanderings around the neighborhood, and it becomes too easy to put off or skip workouts. A vague goal of "fitness" is a difficult one to stay focused on. Fit for what? Fit to look better, or to win an Olympic medal? There are just too many variations on the word. But if your goal is to be fit enough to finish a particular 10K, or to improve your weekly mileage, or to lose pounds, then that focus will really help you get out the door on those days when early-parenthood inertia threatens to take over.

What about those awful days when no help is available and you absolutely must get your run in? The best investment we've made in this regard is a good treadmill. Gail has gotten in many workouts on this machine that otherwise would have disappeared. While the babies slept, she'd hop on the treadmill in our basement, with the room monitor nearby, and get in about 5 miles before they woke up.

Many use baby joggers, those elaborate strollers that you often see parents pushing down the street. We've never owned one. Our hometown of Sherborn, Massachusetts, is a beautiful place to run, but its narrow country roads are winding, bumpy and highly cambered; these aren't ideal conditions for safe use of a baby jogger. Plus, I've seen parents jogging along on a hot summer day, seemingly oblivious to the little sunburned body in the stroller in front of them, or running down a crowded street with auto exhaust fumes belching in the poor child's face. But if you have safe, shaded neighborhood streets to run on, these strollers might work well for you.

Another good solution is early morning running. If Gail knows that she has a busy day ahead, and that I'll be leaving for the day before she can get a run in at normal times, she'll try to get up and out the door by 5:30 A.M., then be back and showered before everyone wakes up. This takes some effort, and it can be dangerous when it's dark or cold, but it's a great feeling to have the early morning roads to yourself and to know that you have the rest of the day to do whatever needs to be done.

Other running parents with whom I've talked rely on the long jump pit solution; that is, put the children with their shovels and pails in the sand in the center of a track, and do your laps while keeping a watchful eye on them. I even have one acquaintance who, upon finding himself a single parent, constructed an eighth-of-a-mile path around his yard. The children could look out the window and see him pass every 45 seconds or so, and he could watch them, too.

But no sooner will you have figured out how to keep in shape while caring for your little ones than will they not be so little anymore, and the rules will have changed again. This is where the real fun begins, namely, doing sports with your children rather than in spite of them. It's a kind of imposed crosstraining that has given new life to an otherwise sometimes dull program of 30- to 40-minute daily runs.

For example, when our older daughter needed swimming lessons, Gail decided to go, too. In 3 months, she progressed from being a slow paddler to being able to swim 1 to 2 miles at a time. That same summer, when our younger daughter aspired to greatness on figure skates, Gail noticed an adult class at the other end of the rink, and she thought that it would be better to participate than to sit around on the ice. She fell on her face the first time, but within 5 months was landing jumps and, at the age of 44, found herself in a state of renewed youthfulness and rejuvenation of her previously tedious workout program.

If you're creative and flexible, running and fitness within the constraints of parenthood are not only possible, but also highly enjoyable. When we packed away the little pink dresses and baby toys for the last time, Gail didn't count the number of workouts that she had missed, but how she and the girls had lived and loved by spending active time together.

If you work standard office hours, there are three obvious choices: before work, sometime during work (most likely in the middle of the day) and after work. Your first step in deciding when to go is to rule out the times you know you can't go. If your office doesn't have a shower, and your midday break is 30 minutes and not negotiable, running then isn't an option. If, however, you can explain to your employer the importance of what you want to do, and tangibly demonstrate not only that it won't interfere with your work, but that running at lunchtime will likely make you a better worker, this can be a great time to run. You don't have to worry about running in the dark, you might be able to have others from work join you, you'll return to your afternoon work refreshed, you'll have plenty of time for other responsibilities before and after work, and, other than in the summer, you're likely to be running in the best weather of the day. When I was teaching school while training for the 1976 Olympics, I received permission to run at lunchtime. Although the school's administration eventually soured on the idea (they told me that I should devote more time to my vocation and less time to my avocation), I certainly enjoyed running in the middle of the day more than getting up and running 10 miles before school in the dark.

Most people, though, are going to have to choose between running before or after work. For many busy people, morning is the better choice, because getting up earlier than you otherwise would means you're not taking away from time in which anybody else might place demands on you. Studies have found that morning exercisers, especially among beginners, are more consistent in their training—there's less chance the work day will spill over into errands will spill over into family time will spill over into dinner, and so on, suddenly making it seem as if there's no time to run. And as I hope that I've drummed into you by now, consistency is the key to improving your running.

At the same time, running after work can be a wonderful way to relieve the workday's stress. Also, most of the physiological processes involved in distance running operate at a higher level in late afternoon than in early morning. This is especially important if you're doing regular speed work, because the quality—and probably the quantity—of your fast running just won't be as good early in the morning. If it's practical to do so, a great trick is to treat your evening run as the final part of your workday, and run from your office. This makes it more likely you'll get in the habit of starting your run at close to the same time most days, and, unlike when you go home and then try to run, you won't be distracted by things such as the mail, the phone, the television, the children and so on. Many people report that it's a great feeling to head home knowing that both their work and their running are done for the day, and that the rest of the evening is theirs to do with as they please.

Louise Kent: The "Re-Creational" Runner

When you first talk to Louise Kent about her running, you think that she's being falsely modest. Louise, of Charlestown, Massachusetts, says, "I'm really just a recreational runner." But Louise works for Nike, and she looks as if she just does it about 4 hours a day—she's 5'4" and weighs a sculpted 105 pounds, and at age 32 she's a 2:56 marathoner. Recreational, indeed, you think. But let her tell her story, and you'll come to agree with her.

Louise's running has had many emphases since she started in ninth grade. Then, it was to get in shape for field hockey. In college, it was initially to combat a 30-pound weight gain in her first year. Then, in her junior and senior years, it was to join her friends on the school's cross country and track teams. Once in the workaday world, it was to relieve stress and to live a healthful lifestyle. Now, it's to compete in the marathon. Yet, one thing has been constant—Louise's pure love of the act of running. Recreation literally means to "re-create," and this is what running does for Louise. "It's invigorating," she says. "It's my own space, my own time, when I'm just out there letting my thoughts go. It's a part of my day like eating, and it's one of my favorite parts."

Louise often runs twice a day, and while her mileage combined with her genes—her father had been a star on his college's team—allows her to race well, competition isn't her main motivation (as much as she admits to liking the feeling of winning). "If I run in the morning before work," she says, "I have a better outlook during the day. I'm ready to dive into my work rather than being sluggish. Then, when I get home from work, it seems the best way to wind down the day."

As further evidence that her potentially intimidating racing success is secondary to running for running's sake, consider her experiences with more systematic training. After she and others noticed her talent for running long races, Louise began to attend a running club's weekly track workouts. "I hated it," she says bluntly. "It was so structured—it took all the fun away from it. Same thing when I tried a heart rate monitor. I felt myself watching the monitor instead of just being out there enjoying my run. I run just as fast without one, but because that's what I feel like doing. I felt like a rat wearing the monitor." So Louise does no speed work, and only runs with others on an occasional long run, which she views "more as a social thing than a structured workout."

"In retrospect, I realize that I've always loved to run," she adds. "In high school, we would run a lot in preseason for field hockey and lacrosse, and I remember being really into being on the team. But once we started playing, I hated it. The running before practice was always better than the sport I was doing it to get ready for."

Ultimately, when to run is going to come down to when works best for you on a regular basis. Make it easiest for fitting it in with everything else that you have to do. And don't be afraid to make good use of the weekends, especially if you're on a moderate program. Say you're running four times a week. If you know that you can get in a run on both weekend days, that means that you have to figure out when to find the time on only two of every five workdays.

TRAINING PARTNERS AND RUNNING CLUBS

Once, Alberto Salazar and I were running through the suburbs of Boston when a Great Dane ran menacingly toward us. The dog ignored me and went straight for Alberto. (Who knows why, other than that Alberto weighs a bit more than I do and has a bit more meat to offer.) Fortunately, I was carrying my keys and was able to use them to scare the dog away. Other than that incident, there have been few times in my 30 years of running that I haven't thought, "The more, the merrier." Training with others is one of the greatest pleasures there is in running and, for that matter, life. It's also one of the most important things you can do to keep running for a lifetime, and to more easily weave running into the fabric of your life.

For me, running has always been a social activity. I started in high school with my brother and best friend, and in college I had a great time with my teammates Amby Burfoot and Jeff Galloway. When I returned to running in the early '70s, I bumped into a few runners almost right away. Within 6 months of returning to running, I had met someone to run with at least twice a week, and within my first year back I joined the Boston Athletic Association. When I moved close to Boston College, several of the runners who started the Greater Boston Track Club lived nearby, so it was natural for me to start running with them regularly.

It's just a normal part of running to bump into other runners while training or at races and to know that not running by yourself all the time will make it easier and more enjoyable. This is especially true if you've had that experience in the past, such as if you ran on the track team in high school; you just automatically gravitate toward trying to recreate that experience. Having runners of a similar level of ability to train with is especially helpful during speed workouts and long runs.

On the other hand, there are many runners, especially nonracers, who pretty much train on their own all the time. That's fine—that's what fits their schedules. But I'm willing to bet that even these people would come to see the benefits of occasionally running with others. It helps break up the monotony and gives different emphases to your running. Some days, you'll go by yourself, and that's your reflection time and you'll really look forward to carving out some time just to be by yourself. Then you can look forward to the next day's run, when you know that you're going to have company and conversation and moral support, that much more. It's great to have that variety to look forward to so that your running doesn't all seem the same.

Running with others is also a great way to combat that most powerful of forces, inertia. This can be equally true whether you make plans to train with someone before or after work. When that alarm clock goes off, and it's cold and dark outside, and nice and comfortable in your bed, sometimes the only thing that keeps you from rolling over and going back to sleep is knowing that somewhere a friend of yours is fighting the same urges just to meet you for a run. That kind of unspoken mutual support adds a whole dimension to your friendship that likely wouldn't develop if your time together consisted of nothing but occasionally eating dinner together.

And if you've made plans to run with someone after work, knowing you've promised your friend you'll be at a certain place at a certain time can help you focus on your work. We all know how work expands to fill the time you have, and if you tell yourself you'll leave for a run on your own only after a certain project is done, it's more likely the project will spill over into early evening, and suddenly it will seem as if there's not time to run that day. If, on the other hand, you've given your word that you'll meet someone to run at 6:15, then the work will magically get done sooner. Also, if you almost automatically go about finishing your work and getting to where you're going to meet your training partner, you're likely to find that once you get going, you're not as tired as you would have thought had you been sitting by yourself at your desk, contemplating whether you have the time and energy to run that day.

How can you find someone to run with? The two best ways are going to races and joining a running club. You might also be able to meet people at a health club, but it's at races and in a running club that you're most likely to easily hook up with someone who has similar goals and abilities as you. You don't have to be a hardcore competitor to meet other runners these ways. As I mentioned in Chapter 1, for example, if you run 3 miles a day, you could go to a 5K race and run your normal pace, and talk with the people who finish around you. They're probably as eager as you to find someone to run with occasionally.

Notice that I said "someone who has similar goals and abilities as you." It's important that your training partners neither be significantly faster nor slower than you. One of the problems that inexperienced runners have is that they repeatedly get in over their heads. Most of my runs are at a relaxed, conversational pace. You don't want to tag along with someone who runs more than a minute per mile faster than you. For them, it's a workout; for you, it's a race, and if your experience of running with others is that it's always push, push, push, you won't be able to appreciate how enjoyable it is to spend an hour on the roads talking with a friend. Adult fitness runners aren't the only ones who are susceptible to run too hard with others frequently. Many young runners on high school and college teams allow themselves to be carried away by their competitiveness and wind up racing each other nearly every day in practice. When it's time to race, they're spent.

You also don't want to run regularly with someone who is light years slower than you. A few years ago, a study had a wide range of runners run at a 10:00 per mile pace. The researchers found that the fastest runners in the group were the least efficient at this pace. For them, the pace was so much slower than what they were used to that they changed their running form, and actually required more oxygen to run at this pace (what's termed "running economy") than the runners for whom 10:00 pace was more like a regular training pace.

It's okay, and even desirable, if once or twice a week you run with someone who's slightly faster than you; you can count on getting a hard run in on those days, and structure your training around these efforts. It's also not a bad idea to occasionally run with someone who runs a little more slowly than you do, because many runners, especially veterans, tend to run too hard on what should be their easy days. If you hook up with a friend who runs 30 seconds per mile slower than you, and run at his or her pace rather than making him or her speed up to stay with you, you'll get a true recovery day. You'll then be really rested and ready to nail your tougher days, such as speed workouts and long runs. I run a few times a week with a neighbor, and with him I run slower than I would on my own, but not so much that it's ridiculous. It's nice to know that I'm recovering from my harder training on my own and simultaneously getting in some socializing.

One of the main reasons runners like to train together is because doing so helps them prepare better for races. When I joined the Greater Boston Track Club in the early '70s, I was able to draw on the ability of others who might be better than me in a given area of training. For example, Greg Meyer, who won the Boston Marathon in 1983, was always better at doing track workouts than I was. He just has better natural speed. (At his best, he could run a 4:00 mile, which is excellent short-distance speed for a world-class marathoner.) I knew I couldn't stick with him for an entire track workout, but I would try, and doing so would pull me through most of the workout at a higher level of quality than I would have achieved on my own. The same thing was true when I would do speed work with Alberto Salazar. They could always nail me at the end of a workout, and that was a little depressing, but I would try to draw something positive out of it. I would say to myself, "OK, they're better than me in this area, but maybe I'm more consistent with my mileage, or I'm better at long runs than them. I almost stayed with them on their turf, so when we get to mine, the marathon, I know I should be able to beat them."

The other main type of workout that runners make a special effort to do together is long runs. In these, you don't necessarily want to feel as if you're always being pulled along noticeably faster than you would be on your own; your main goal in these should be to cover the distance without breaking yourself down. Running with others on long runs should be beneficial mostly by the others' presence helping you to run longer than you might on your own. Twelve miles into a 20-miler; it's easier to rationalize why you should cut it short when you're on your own compared to when you're out there with a few friends, talking and inspiring each other to keep going.

That's not to say you should completely ignore how you're feeling. You have to protect your territory when you're training with others. Because of, I suppose, pride, it's easy to be talked into going faster or farther than you had planned when you have company. This is usually tempting, because it can be so much fun to run with others, but don't train to someone else's advantage. I've made this mistake many times. For example, I'll have done a long run the day before, but get talked into doing a track workout because it's the only good time that week for my teammates. Then I drag around for a week. In those cases, evaluate your workout as you go, and don't be afraid to cut it short if you sense you're doing yourself more harm than good. If you're tired from working too much or traveling, or you have a race in a few days, stick to what you have planned.

Like I said, it can really help you improve to occasionally do a distance run or a speed workout with someone who is a bit faster than you. How do you know when it's too fast? Say you're joining a running club at its weekly track workouts, and every week you feel you're in way over your head from step one. If you don't notice improvement after 8 weeks, try to find a different group. You shouldn't be pushing yourself endlessly and aimlessly beyond where you're getting something positive out of your workout.

That's why joining a running club is such a good idea. It's likely there will be small groups of people with a similar level of fitness. You can find the group that best matches your current level, and as you progress, join a faster group if necessary. The same is true of long runs. Many clubs have a standard meeting place and time for weekly long runs; usually, everyone there will break into small groups of people who want to cover the same distance at roughly the same pace. Get there early and ask around about who's doing what, and start with the group whose members most sound like runners who have been training as you've been lately.

In doing so, you're likely to discover one of the greatest things about running with others. You can get out there with a group, and you know one another as runners. The group is probably a mix of ages, genders, classes, occupations and other things that tend to divide people in our society. You'll probably meet people who you would otherwise never know, and, through shared effort, become better friends in a shorter time than you might think possible. I think that's one reason why adult runners seem to be happier than some sedentary people their age. Once you start working fulltime, raising a family, and so on, it becomes very difficult to make new friends. But through running with others, you can keep meeting new people into your 70s and beyond. These days, I train on my own more than I ever have, and I have to admit that I don't enjoy it as much. I really look forward to the one or two runs a week when I can get together with another runner and spend some quality time on the roads.

JUMP-STARTING YOUR RUNNING

We all hit flat patches in our training. Suddenly, running isn't as much fun as it used to be, and although you know that you're going to stick with it, you wish that you could recapture some of the excitement that it seems to lack. I've discussed elsewhere how to get around this inevitable problem on a systematic basis—take a seasonal approach to your running, include a variety of paces and distances when planning your training, run in special locations once in a while, run at different times of the day, run with different people, and, if need be, take a break from running. What I'm talking about in this section, though, is what to do when those day-to-day tweaks don't work, and you need something big to shake things up. I call this "jump-starting" your running.

This is something that long-time runners have to deal with the most. Once you realize that you're not going to PR anymore, it can be tough to keep your running enough of a challenge so that it stays fresh. The same is true if you've set a big goal, such as finishing a marathon, and have reached it. What now? you wonder. I always try to view a change in my situation from a positive perspective. For now, I've retired from the marathon, which is my best event. My focus is now on shorter races, and I run many more 5Ks than I did in my prime. The 5K is far from my best distance, both physically and mentally. I could let this get me down, but instead I emphasize the challenge that's inherent in this—this isn't my best distance, but how fast can I run it? How close to my times of 5 years ago can I run it? If racing is one of your main motivations, as it is for me, you can always find new standards to strive for. Every 5 years, you enter a new age group, and not only can you treat that as a clean slate, but you can also focus on a distance that you almost never ran in your previous age group.

There are other ways to refocus your running that don't involve racing. Trail running is becoming increasingly popular, especially among baby boomers. I think that's because a lot of us raced heavily in our 20s and 30s, when we were at our peak ages for distance running. We know we're not going to PR anymore, and our lives have become very busy, so we don't have the time and energy to focus on reaching our potential like we used to. In trail running, that doesn't matter. The distances are inexact, and comparing times from one course to another is pretty meaningless. This frees you from obsessing over those matters, as you might if you concentrate on 10K road races, and allows you to emphasize the experience, not the outcome. I'm still a road runner at heart, and I probably always will be, but I can understand the satisfaction and enjoyment that comes from getting away from noise and traffic and asphalt and feeling the earth under you in a meditative environment.

For older runners who might be frustrated about not being able to run as much as they'd like, exploring a variety of crosstraining activities can help. You can make running the foundation of your fitness program, but expand the types of exercises you do and enjoy the new challenge of mastering these. As I mentioned in Chapter 4, my wife, Gail, has switched from marathoning to running a few times a week as part of a broad-based fitness program. She really looks forward to her runs now, and she's always setting new goals in her new pursuits. For example, she started weight training to help alleviate lower back pain, but found that she enjoyed it, and got so serious about it that she could benchpress 125

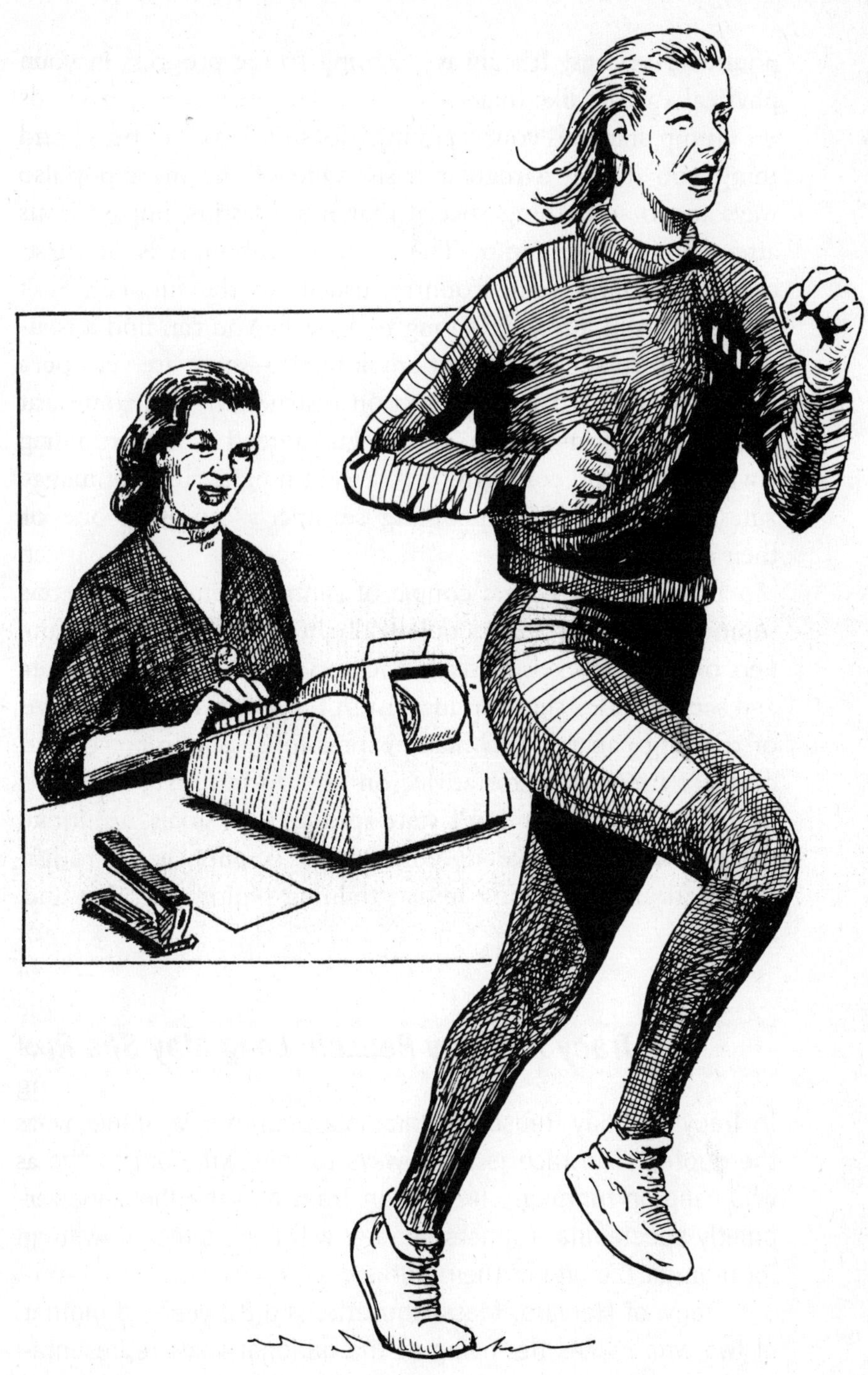

pounds 10 times! It's always exciting to see progress in your physical abilities like that.

Jump-starting your running doesn't have to be something you do on a regular basis. One of the most popular ways to do something special that has a lasting impact is to attend a running camp. There are now hundreds of these camps throughout the country, usually in the summer. Sessions last from a few days long to a week. You can find a running camp to suit just about any interest—some are very performance oriented, some focus on instruction, and some are low-key vacations where you're guaranteed a nice running environment and company, if you want it. The running magazines usually list the upcoming summer's camps in one of their spring issues.

I'm involved with a couple of running camps during the summer, and I see that people really benefit from them. Runners of varying levels of seriousness and ability come together and see that they share an interest in the sport, and that a love of running can take on many expressions. A number of the campers are looking for advice on how to improve; nearly all of them, even if they can't state specific time goals, are looking for ways to make their running go smoother through information on avoiding injury, training philosophy, diet and so on.

Tracy Halliday Reusch: Long May She Run

In Tracy Halliday Reusch's office is a picture of a runner with the quote, "The race is not always to the swift, but to those who keep on running." If so, then Tracy and the thousands of quietly spectacular runners like her will have a medal waiting for them at the end of their journey.

Tracy, of Harvard, Massachusetts, is a 32-year-old mother of two who makes her living as the national sales representative for a magazine. On the surface, she seems like any other 30-something parent who tries to juggle career, family and a long commute. There's one main difference, though: Tracy is an ultramarathoner. In 1995, she ran eight marathons, a 50-mile race and a 90-mile run. The previous year, she ran a trail 100-miler. Suffice it to say that she boldly goes where few women in her life situation go.

But multihour treks were far from her mind when she began running regularly in the spring of 1990. A year after the birth of her older daughter, Tracy returned from a cruise and didn't like what she saw in photos from the trip. "I was never thin," she says, "but this was disgusting." At 5'3", Tracy's weight had bulged to 158. "I was disgusted with myself," she remembers. So she started running 2 miles a day, 4 times a week, and watching her diet. Her goal was to get down to 125 pounds by that July; she reached 120.

"One day that summer, I tried to run as long as I could," Tracy says. "I went nine miles and was amazed. I felt incredible during and after, and I had this incredible sense of accomplishment." With more miles came a different emphasis to her running. "Running gave me a new identity," she says. "I started to learn about myself, to feel more confident about myself, and that carried over to other parts of my life."

After her second daughter was born in the fall of 1991, Tracy began running with others who were focused on the Boston Marathon. Tracy made her marathon debut there in 1993, running 4:12 and finding "a real camaraderie among the runners." Enticed by the fun of it all, Tracy volunteered as a pacer for a competitor in the Vermont 100-miler that summer. "I was amazed by these people who could run for so long," she says, "and I decided that I would try to run a longer race." That fall, she ran two 50-milers and, she says, "fell in love with long races."

The important thing to remember about Tracy is that she handles these races easily on minimal mileage. "On a good week, I'll run six times," she says, "but most of those are four or five-milers." Only on the rare uncluttered weekend does she have the time for the 3-hour runs that most ultra runners do like clockwork. Not counting the long races, she rarely does more than 40 miles a week. Tracy shows that a big heart and a strong head can overcome many of the constraints that a busy schedule can place on runners who try to reach for the stars.

"Everyone is capable of doing this," she claims. "I'm not unique. The main thing to me is to enjoy my running, just like it is for most people. Those long, slow runs—that's my time, my time to think. People shouldn't be intimidated by what I do. I'm just out there learning who I am."

I try to make these camps as fun as possible while still imparting worthwhile information. There are some camps at which your whole day is focused on the next run, an end-of-the-week race, and so on. We get our running in, and many people run more at camp than they usually do on their own, but I don't want these camps to be a grind. You can make running as much of a grind as you want on your own! I want people to come away with the opposite view. I'm usually joined at camp by Joan Benoit Samuelson. I want people to leave camp with the feeling, "OK, this is what she does with her training, and she's got two little kids like I do. What do her kids think about her running? How does she do it? What does she do that I can apply to my situation? And what does she really eat?" Months after being at camp, you can focus on what you learned there, and apply it in new ways to keep your running fresh.

RUNNING WHILE TRAVELING

In the fall of 1992 I was in Caracas, Venezuela doing clinics before the Marathon of Caracas. One morning, I woke to the sound of popping noises. The national election was coming up, so I thought I was hearing firecrackers. My brother Charlie and I went to the hotel lobby to take a cab to a park to run, but we were told, "No cabs today—shooting in the streets." It turned out that a coup to overthrow the government was underway, and the popping noise I had heard was gunfire! Worse yet, my hotel was the headquarters for the government's counterattack. Two hundred or so of us crawled down into the hotel restaurant and spent about 6 hours lying on the floor while jets flew by and nervous kids with machine guns came in and out. Two soldiers were killed

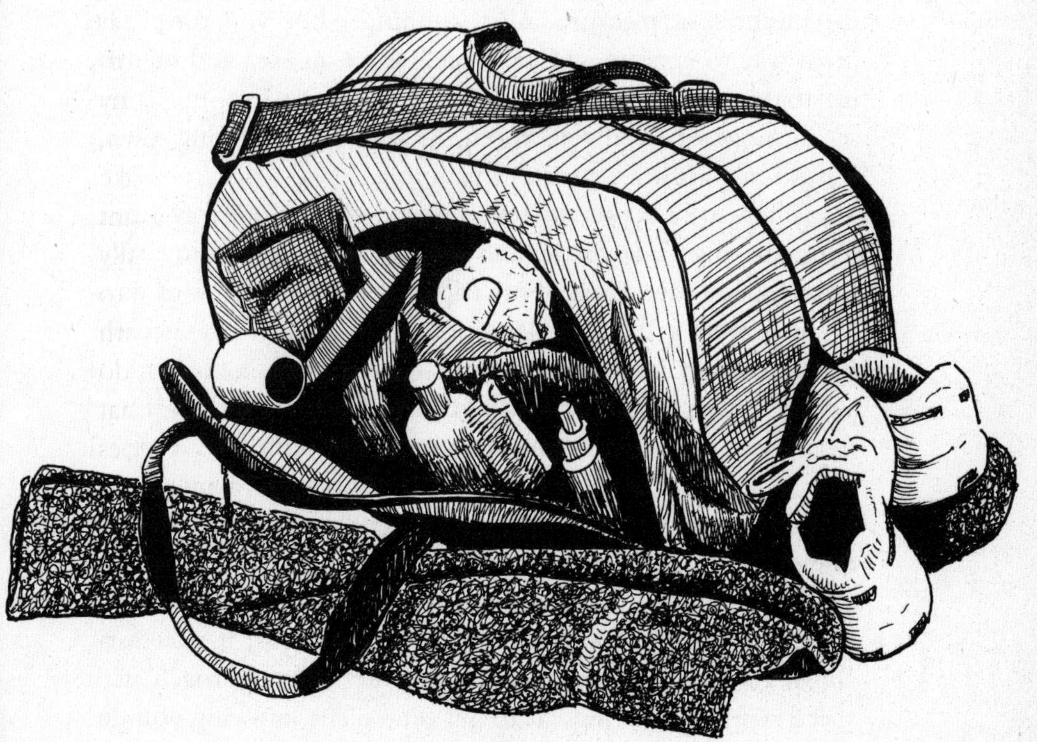

on the hotel grounds. Running suddenly didn't seem all that important.

The coup only lasted one day. The next day, the streets were still not safe, but one of the race officials got me a pass to get on to the air base that was half a mile away so I could run there. Ironically, this was where the coup had been launched from.

This incident is admittedly an extreme example, but it underscores a fundamental fact about running while traveling: it can be difficult, but if you maintain a flexible approach, it is almost always doable. In fact, I meet people all the time who tell me the same thing: running helps them to be better travelers. They find that even just a short run when they arrive at a new locale helps the fatigue of travel melt away, wakes them up, boosts their appetite, and helps them sleep better, so the next day they can accomplish more, whether they're traveling for business or pleasure. Also, running while you travel is a great way to explore and get a feeling for an area and its people that you can't get riding around in a tour bus, much less secluding yourself in your room. As with most running, doing it right takes just a little bit of planning.

There are two key matters to tend to for your travel running: making time for it, and finding a good running spot. First, scheduling. Most of my trips last from one to four days. If I'm traveling to race, planning my training is easy, because I'll be cutting back, so fitting it in isn't really a concern. If I'm not racing, I try to plan my training around my travel schedule. I often do a long run on the morning of a trip; I hate to get on a plane and either arrive home or, worse, at an unfamiliar location and still have to get my run in. Also, by doing a long run on the first day of a trip, you've earned an easy training day for the next day, and this gives you extra time and energy to recover from traveling and, if necessary, adjust to time zone changes. I use the same approach with speed workouts—it's great to get on a plane knowing you got in a good effort earlier in the day and can relax for the rest of the day.

For many runners, vacation is a chance to luxuriate in some extra training. You're away from all the responsibilities of work and home, so with a little schedule coordination, you should really be able to indulge yourself. If you're traveling with your family, work things out with others. Everyone usually has something they want to do on their own, so exchange time with them to make time for your running. For example, if your spouse wants to go swimming and you want to run, switch off watching the children while allowing each other some time alone. The morning is the easiest time to do this. You get your running out of the way and have the rest of the day to do "regular" vacation activities with everyone.

The key thing once you've arrived is finding good running spots. This can take some work, so once you know a city, try to arrange things so that, if you return, you can get back to a familiar locale. For example, when I travel to New York City, I always make sure I stay near Central Park—it has a 6-mile loop, and you can't ask for much more than that from such a crowded place. Ask around about parks, lakes and rivers; these usually have some sort of path that you can get in some miles on. There are also guidebooks to running in various cities that can be very helpful if you're often on the road, and with so many people walking and running today, many hotels provide maps for nearby running paths. Remember, though, you might have to improvise. Many nonrunners aren't good at accurately assessing distance. They might tell you about a great park to run in that might be all of 200 yards around; that's not my idea of enjoyable running! One of the great things about our sport is that it's so portable, so if others' suggestions don't work out, you can strike out on your own and usually find someplace decent to run. When in doubt, use relatively straight, out-and-back courses, on which you're less likely to get lost.

Sometimes, though, you just have to make the best of a bad situation. When I was in São Paulo, Brazil, there was really nowhere to run. I finally found a small park that was maybe 600 yards in circumference, and I just resigned myself to the drudgery of running there. Ho Chi Minh City, in Vietnam, was the most crowded place I've ever run—there were people all over the streets selling things, riding bikes, motorcycles, carts. I wound up doing most of my running at the local zoo, and even that was dangerous.

This emphasizes one of the most important points about running while traveling: you have to remain flexible. Don't freak out if things don't go as planned. You might find yourself with the wrong clothing, or your luggage might have gotten lost. Although you can do much to prevent these occurrences, such as by checking the weather ahead and keeping some of your running gear in your carry-on luggage, you always have to be adaptable. Before the 1976 New York City Marathon, I was staying with a friend in town. I woke up the morning of the race to find that I hadn't packed any running shorts! I wound up borrowing a pair of soccer shorts from a kid next door, and was still able to win the race.

When you're traveling in conjunction with a race, it's nice to have most of your spare time after the race. You have to sacrifice a certain part of your life to that pre-race rest ritual, and this restricts your ability to get out and enjoy the area you're in. This is especially so before a long race, which is what most of the running vacations available are packaged around. If you run your race at the beginning of your trip, you'll probably not be running much for a few days after anyway; this makes it easier for your schedule to mesh with others'.

Remember, running is supposed to be a fun part of your life. Don't ruin your travel by letting it take over your day. After I ran the world cross country championships in Morocco in 1975, our team had a 5-day stay in Spain. I was really focused on my training—it was only a month before my big breakthrough at the Boston Marathon—and all I did was run twice a day and otherwise stay in my hotel room. Others went to art museums and all the other sights the area had to offer. Even though I wouldn't trade my race at the 1975 Boston Marathon for anything, to this day I regret not making more of the opportunity to see Spain, because that was the only time I've been there. You never know if you're going to get back to an area, so take advantage of it while you're there.

Passing the Torch

CHILDREN'S AND CHARITY RUNNING

Children should learn that it's a natural part of your day to get outside and do something aerobic, that you want to be thinking about maintaining decent muscular strength and flexibility your whole life, and that crashing on the couch in front of the television isn't how we're designed to spend our Saturday afternoons.

If you ask my younger daughter what I do, she'll tell you that I'm the fastest runner in the world. In other words, she doesn't know much about running. Neither she nor her sister know Frank Shorter from Frank Perdue. Both are preteens, so this is how it should be. If they want to get into running, it should be on their own terms. I discovered running without pressure from my parents or other adults, and as a result, I could pursue it on my terms, and allow my love for it to grow genuinely. My wife, Gail, and I want the same for our daughters. Naturally, I would be thrilled if they come to the decision that they want to be runners. At the same time, I'm careful that my admitted immersion in the sport not be their only, or even main, concept of what running is.

In this chapter, we'll look at how to get children to view running as a positive, fun force in their lives while laying the groundwork for it to become a lifetime sport. Inculcating a genuine love of running and fitness is one of the greatest gifts you can give your children and, by extension, society. We'll also look at other ways that you can use your running to benefit others.

WHY SHOULD CHILDREN RUN?

This isn't a rhetorical question. As you'll see, I'm certainly not in favor of junior high and elementary school children being involved in a systematic running program. At the same time, despite their parents having come to age during the fitness boom of the past 20 years, American children today are more unhealthy than ever. A few scary stats: the average teenager watches 22 hours of television a week. That might not sound like much (maybe you watch more!), but it adds to nearly one day of the week spent passively plopped in front of the tube. Many studies have shown a direct relation between the time a child spends watching television and his or her body fat percentage. If you think a child's body fat percentage is unimportant, consider this: 40 percent of children between the ages of 5 and 8 are obese and have elevated blood pressure and cholesterol levels. Only one-third of children ages 6 to 17 meet minimum standards for cardiovascular fitness. The more out of shape a child is, the less likely it is that he or she will be active enough to explore fitness options. This early inactivity has long-term effects: girls who aren't active in sports by age 10 have only a 10 percent chance of being involved in sports at age 25.

So it's imperative that children be active from as early an age as possible. Gail and I like to expose our daughters to as many activities as possible. Our girls like to skate, run, dance, play basketball and tennis—they're pretty well-rounded, and don't concentrate on any one activity. The running they do is mostly in play and as part of doing other sports, and that's how it should be for preteens. Child psychologists say most preteens haven't yet developed their capacity for abstract thinking; as you've probably experienced, this means it's hard to motivate them with long-term goals, especially ones achieved through delayed gratification. In running terms, this means that children of this age aren't going to understand some of the core concepts of training, such as suffering some in the present (training hard) so they won't suffer as much in the future (racing well). Children who are eager to compete at these ages aren't likely to grasp what's involved, and they're likely to get frustrated and turned off by running because quantifying success can be so tricky. Having a child burnt out on running before puberty is hardly the way to instill a lifelong love of the sport!

You want the best for your children, right? You wouldn't purposefully skimp on their education, because you know how important that is for the rest of their lives. Their fitness should get the same respect. For whatever reason—perhaps by dumb luck—you were fortunate enough to learn what a profound impact running and fitness can have on your life, and you know how important good habits and the proper mindset are. Why wouldn't you want your children to learn these valuable lessons as well? And why wouldn't you want to do what you can to help them learn, rather than leave it to chance?

HOW SHOULD CHILDREN RUN?

Common sense has to be the guiding principle in children's running. I see no future benefits, and probably some negatives, for those who are intensely involved in age-group competition. With a few exceptions, you just don't see those people carry on with their running into high school and college and beyond, when they're finally mature enough to compete near their potential. Performance aside, they give up on running just as they're entering the stage of their lives when it could help them the most.

Before the age of 14, I believe that children should take part in as wide a range of activities as possible. This achieves several purposes. First, it simply exposes them to what's out there. As you've discovered with your running, the key to staying fit for a lifetime is to find that activity or those activities that you *want* to do, not that you think you *have* to do. How are children going to know what might be for them if their introduction to sport is limited to baseball or intense, age-group running competition?

Second, a well-rounded dabbling in activities imparts the idea that fitness is a lifestyle, not just something that's freakish and separate from the rest of your life or that you haphazardly do. As Gail likes to say, "We don't exercise. We train." This doesn't mean there's a chin-up bar in every doorway in our house or that breakfast is served only after our daughters have dropped and given us 20. Rather, it means we try to impress on them that it's a natural part of your day to get outside and do something aerobic, that you want to be thinking about

maintaining decent muscular strength and flexibility your whole life in the same way you want to read regularly about a variety of topics to keep your mind fit, and that crashing on the couch in front of the television isn't how we're designed to spend our Saturday afternoons.

Finally, it's just a good idea for children's fitness development and avoidance of injury to do as many activities as possible while growing. This helps strengthen all of their bones and muscles, and gives them a solid "infrastructure" on which to build when it's OK in their later teens to get more serious about training for one or two sports only. My childhood is illustrative here. I played baseball, basketball, football, hockey, badminton and golf, and I was also active in sledding, ice skating, swimming, fishing, hunting, camping and hiking. (I was a Boy Scout.) I certainly wasn't thinking, "Well, I'll go swimming today, play basketball tomorrow, then play hockey the next day, and in fifteen years I'll win the Boston Marathon." I was just an average kid of my generation growing up and having fun. In retrospect, however, I realize that doing all of these activities instilled a real love for being active outdoors; staying indoors and *not* being outside in motion seemed the foreign thing to me, not the opposite, as it is to many children today. The activities of my childhood probably also helped me build a balanced, strong body that could handle the load when I moved toward specializing in one sport, running, and gradually increased my mileage and intensity. And as my body was able to absorb more work, so was my mind, because it hadn't become burnt out from fierce concentration on attaining specific performance goals when I was 12 years old.

It was through this everything-and-the-kitchen-sink way of being active outdoors while growing up that I stumbled onto running. The Newington, Connecticut Parks and Recreation Department would put on summer games programs, and one of the events was a small track meet. I decided that I would run the longest race, the mile. I won on the 5-lap grass track in 5:20 and became excited enough about running to join the high school cross country team with my brother, Charlie, and best friend, Jason Kehoe. Even then, everything was still low-key. We had only three races that fall and we were a non-varsity sport. We didn't care. We had great fun and team spirit, and our coach, Frank O'Rourke, always treated us to ice cream after our meets. How could we not fall in love with the sport? So many years later, the three of us are still running strong. I firmly believe that our gradual introduction to running as something fun, after a childhood of sampling every conceivable activity, is the main reason why.

If your child sees you running and expresses a desire to run with you, by all means go ahead, but understand that even "fit" kids have to be accustomed to running long distances. Don't expect—or encourage—them to go more than 2 or 3 miles or 20 to 30 minutes at a time. Let the runs unfold on the child's terms. That might mean stopping and walking, exploring something by the side of the road, turning around and heading home after just a few minutes, etc. Whatever you do, don't turn it into a hard workout. "Having fun" consistently ranks as the main reason that, when polled, children say that they participate in sports. As I said in Chapter 3, there are many definitions of fun, and for adults who know their goals and can say why they do what they do, this can certainly involve the seemingly perverse fun of training hard, pushing toward a long-term target, and so on. For children, though, fun means primarily enjoying the here and now. Your child won't view running as fun if he or she associates it with being out of breath from step one while you run a few steps ahead and challenge him or her to keep up with you. Like I said, let the child dictate the run. Stay beside, or a step or two behind, so that he or she feels as if there's no competition involved.

You probably won't be surprised, then, to read that I don't think that children under the age of 18 should run marathons. There's just no real benefit to be had, and the risks of getting burnt out and injured are so great. Adults have a hard enough time being able to articulate why they want to attempt such a crazy distance. It's likely that children who express a desire to run the marathon don't really understand what's involved in the preparation, in running the race and in recovering from it. They probably think that they're invincible. (My coauthor wishes that we had written this book 15 years ago, when he ran his first marathon, the 1981 Baltimore Marathon, as a high school senior and ruined most of the rest of his year in interscholastic races. Incidentally, I was at that event, and signed an autograph for Scott the night before the race. That's one of the great things we all share as runners—you never know how your paths are going to end up crossing.)

I'm not suggesting that teens can't run some impressive marathons. For example, Golden Harper, of Orem, Utah, ran 2:44 at the 1995 St. George Marathon *at the age of 13!* This is a wonderful achievement, and Golden comes from a running family (his mother has run 2:39), so he probably has good training knowledge and does all the right things in terms of diet, sleep, etc. Still, there's no way that he can do his best in the event at such a young age. More important, children who are serious enough about running to be contemplating the marathon would be better served, both short-term and long-term, by focusing their attention on scholastic competition. Training for and racing the marathon are obviously going to detract from their ability to maximize their potential in the more traditional teen distances of the mile and 2-mile. Children have the rest of their lives to run long road races. How many chances are they going to get as adults to develop their short-distance speed to its fullest? You can always move up in distance. Getting that good speed base when you're young really contributes to your success at all distances once you're in your 20s and beyond and are physically and mentally mature enough to really explore your distance running potential.

THE RIGHT RUNNING EVENTS FOR CHILDREN

It's not that I'm against children participating in road races. But they should be special kinds of road races. In recent years, road racing has increased its efforts to be kid-friendly. Now, many races have separate children's fun runs held in conjunction with the main events. These usually are a mile or shorter in distance, and they start and finish before the adult race, so parents can watch and encourage their children, and sometimes run with them. On the past few Thanksgivings, for example, I've run the Feaster Five Mile Race in Andover, Massachusetts. When my older daughter was 8 years old, she decided she wanted to run the "Kids' K," a one-kilometer run for children. She ran it (wearing her winter coat!) and was very pleased, as was I, when she received her medal along with all of the kids who ran. This is how it should be. Children's fun runs should give something to everyone who finishes, rather than prizes for the top few. Acknowledging all of the participants better gets across the idea that the real accomplishment is taking part, not winning. This helps encourage the slower children to keep coming back and to view running as a sport that's for everyone, not just the elite. I'm not as interested that my daughters become great racers as I am that they learn about what running might offer them and what it means to live your life being fit.

Some of the children's runs have taken on a life of their own. The Bloomsday Road Race, a 12K held in Spokane, Washington, holds a 2-mile kids' run called the Junior Bloomsday. They get more than 6,000 children to run! Perhaps my favorite children's run was one I attended in Ohio. Not only were the kids running the race, but they were also running the show—they started the race, gave out water and encouragement along the route, supplied music at the start/finish area, etc. It was a great thing to see.

As encouraging as the growing popularity of these types of events is, more could be done. Participation is always random, mostly based on if a child's parents are running the "real" race. We need to devise ways to get more kids involved. My guess is that nearly every elementary, middle and senior high school in the country has at least one staff member who is a runner, walker or some other type of aerobic exerciser.

Wouldn't it be great if every school had a weeklong seminar on fitness, good health and how to prepare for a 1-mile run? Every school could have speakers come in to talk to the students on preparing for a race and to answer questions. I do many such school appearances and have always found the kids to be very curious about the Olympics, the marathon, running shoes and gear, what prizes you can win, and what it means to be fit in an aerobic sense. The interest is definitely there; we just need to devise systematic ways to nurture it. We need to bring sports medicine physicians, physical therapists and nutritionists to our schools to expose our children to the positive information about health and exercise that they need to fend off the barrage of misinformation that comes at them from the sports pages, television and the fast food industries.

A big hindrance to this is what I call the "school factor," namely, which sports are encouraged by our society. Unfortunately, it's mostly the fast-twitch, anaerobic sports that require short bursts of speed but little or no endurance. These aren't the kinds of sports that are going to keep you healthy for a lifetime. Also, our schools don't adequately encourage mass participation by the students. Instead, the talented few are chosen to be participants, and everyone else is relegated to the role of spectator. Once set in childhood, these ways of viewing sports are hard to break out of, so most adults are fans rather than athletes.

I'd like to see schools linked with their community's running clubs. Runners from the club could speak to the students about running and help them to prepare for a local race. Almost every town has some sort of road race; can you imagine the impact on future fitness and children's lifelong habits if every school in the country fielded "teams" of their students at local races? I've seen this done at the CowTown 10K, in Fort Worth, Texas, where thousands of kids run each year.

Another approach is offered by an event that I've become involved with called Fitness University. It's been conducted by the Nashua (New Hampshire) Striders since the late 1980s. Club members go into local elementary and middle schools and recruit children to join them at club practices once a week. There the children see the adults, discuss how to build their running, and how to eat healthfully. After 6 weeks of this, they have "Finals Day." About 1,000 kids come to the local track and take part in races while their parents watch from the stands. Each child gets a medal and certificate, as well as food and drink with their schoolmates and friends. I ran a lot of the runs with the kids, as did the Nashua Striders, and you could see the satisfaction in the children's faces. This should be developed into a national program. Skip Cleaver, the organizer of the event, gets sponsorship from Healthsource, a local HMO, but we need a national company with a strong interest in the health and well-being of our country's youth.

One aspect of the program is the Road Runners Club of America Running Development Program, which they have funded in more than 100 RRCA clubs. They have produced a 20-page booklet, "Children's Running: A Guide for Parents and Kids," to distribute in schools via RRCA clubs. They also have a 62-page curriculum guide for the teacher. (See the appendix for information on how to order these guides.) At this writing, about 9,000 of the curriculum guides have been distributed. There are still 20,000 copies available. I would love to see a company step forward to fund the distribution of these copies to help tie the 600-plus clubs of the RRCA into schools across the country. We need innovative approaches such as this to overcome the structural barriers to getting all children exercising that exist in our current sports system.

I know we savor and cultivate the star system of athletics in the U.S., but we lose more than we gain by this approach. Certainly the entire student body should be far more heavily encouraged and supported by parents, teachers, coaches and media to explore a wide range of sports, particularly those that are healthful, lifetime sports. Running fits that description well!

RUNNING AND CHARITIES

Runners who pass on their love of running to their children have done society a great good. There's another major way that I think more runners should become involved in bettering society, and that's by becoming involved in the increasing number of running events that are tied to fund raising for a charity.

I've always had a sympathy for those who are less fortunate than I am. I had a cousin who had cerebral palsy and was retarded, and my maternal grandmother had multiple sclerosis. I was a special education teacher, and I've since become regularly involved with the Special Olympics. I'm an old sociology major from the '60s, so maybe I'm a bit off, but I'm always looking for ways to see how running can affect our society for the better. Fortunately, others do, too, and now there are organized running events and programs that make it easy for runners to make a difference. Two well-known examples are the Race for the Cure series, which raises money for breast cancer research, and Team in Training, a marathon training program in which participants get pledges before running a marathon for money for leukemia research.

I do my small part by putting on a series of short fun runs in December in the Boston area. These Jingle Bell Runs are noncompetitive, 2½ to 3 mile runs; the participants collect pledges for the Special Olympics. I like the fun nature of these events. I just out and out love to see people having a great time, and it seems that nearly everyone does. At the largest one, held in downtown Boston a week or so before Christmas, we get more than 4,000 runners and walkers every year.

Most of them wear some sort of holiday costume, and I'm always delighted to see this huge crowd moving comfortably through the streets of Boston on a Sunday night having fun and making the world a better place at the same time. This event alone raises about $150,000 a year. Afterward, we all pile into the grand ballroom of the Boston Sheraton to eat, drink and dance, and to see the Massachusetts chapter of the Special Olympics receive this big donation.

If I had to choose one running event that I'll always be most honored to be associated with, it wouldn't be the Boston or New York City Marathons. It would be these Jingle Bell Runs. It really helps you put things in perspective and to be more appreciative of what you have. It's important that runners not stand apart from the rest of the world. Instead, as with weaving running into the fabric of your life, we should always be thinking about how to integrate the many positive aspects of our sport into the rest of society. We see so many intractable negatives in our society today; here's something where you can make a difference while having fun and doing what you would be doing anyway.

RESOURCES FOR RUNNERS

PUBLICATIONS

American Track & Field
Shooting Star Media
583 D'Onofrio Drive, Suite 203
Madison, WI 53719
Phone: 608–827–0806; Fax: 608–827–0811

This quarterly magazine focuses on training information for competitive track and field athletes. Many of the articles are written from a coach's perspective, but there are also profiles of leading high school, collegiate and open track and field competitors. Young runners will appreciate the healthy amount of attention given to scholastic track and field.

FootNotes
411 Park Lane
Champaign, IL 61820
Phone: 217–359–9644; Fax: 217–359–4731; E-Mail: Joe Seeley@nova.novanet.org

This is the quarterly publication of the Road Runners Club of America. Most of its articles are targeted toward grassroots running—trends in running, club administration, book reviews, issues in road racing, etc. RRCA members receive *FootNotes* as part of their membership.

National Masters News
P.O. Box 50098
Eugene, OR 97405
Phone: 503-343-7716; Fax: 503-345-2436

Competitive masters will love this monthly newspaper-format publication. Much of it is reports and results from age-group track and field meets. It also includes in-depth coverage of masters road racing, training and injury advice and age-group records listings and other stats.

Race Results Weekly
P.O. Box 7388, FDR Station
New York, NY 10150
Phone: 212-794-3849; Fax: 212-794-3849; E-mail: dfmonti@pipeline.com

This weekly newsletter delivers deep open and age-group results of leading road races and international track meets. It's primarily a results-only, prose-free publication that is sent to subscribers by fax or e-mail by Monday mornings, just 24 hours after most events are held.

Runner's World
33 East Minor St.
Emmaus, PA 18098
Phone: 610-967-8322; Fax: 610-967-7793; E-mail: runnerswdm@aol.com; Web page: http://www.runnersworld.com

This monthly magazine is the largest running publication in the world. It contains advice on training, nutrition, injury, crosstraining and running gear. It also includes athlete profiles, a race calendar and race results. Most of the training advice is geared toward beginning and intermediate runners.

Running & FitNews
4405 East West Highway, Suite 405
Bethesda, MD 20814
Phone: 301–913–9517; Fax: 301–913–9520

This monthly newsletter is the publication of the American Running and Fitness Association. It reports on recent advances in sports medicine, exercise science and nutrition. It also contains many articles on injury treatment and prevention. All of the articles are reviewed by an editorial board of sports medicine professionals. ARFA members receive *Running & FitNews* as part of their membership.

Running, Ranting, Racing
7327 Green Oak Terrace
Lanham, MD 20706
Phone: 301–552–2252

This monthly newsletter contains race reports and opinion pieces on the state of American distance running. It's written from an insider's viewpoint and is irreverent, satirical and amusing.

Running Research News
P.O. Box 27041
Lansing, MI 48909
Phone: 517–371–4897; Fax: 517–371–4447

This newsletter comes out 6 times a year. It reports on recent exercise science research and shows how to apply these findings to improving your running. Its main target audience is serious road racers.

Running Stats
1085 14th Street
Boulder, CO 80302
Fax: 303–494–1362; Web page:
http://rainbow.rmii.com/~benjid/rs.html

This four-page newsletter comes out 44 times per year. It provides results and reports from world-class road, track and cross-country races. It also contains news on elite athletes and races.

Running Times
98 North Washington St.
Boston, MA 02114
Phone: 617–367–2228; Fax: 617–367–2350; E-mail:
rtjparker@aol.com

This magazine comes out 10 times per year. It contains training, nutrition and sports medicine advice, race calendars and results, scholastic running reports and running shoe and apparel reviews. Bill Rodgers is a contributing editor.

Track & Field News
2570 El Camino Real, Suite 606
Mt. View, CA 94040
Phone: 415–948–8188; Fax: 415–948–9445

This monthly magazine contains extensive coverage of track and field and cross country at the high school through professional levels. It regularly includes world, U.S., collegiate and high school rankings at all distances.

ORGANIZATIONS

American College of Sports Medicine
P.O. Box 144
Indianapolis, IN 46206
Phone: 317–637–9200

This is a professional organization whose members are primarily sports medicine and exercise science professionals. It regularly disseminates information to the public on the latest in exercise science and nutrition based on the research of its members. Members receive *Medicine & Science in Sports & Exercise*, a monthly, peer-reviewed publication of recent research.

American Running and Fitness Association
4405 East West Highway, Suite 405
Bethesda, MD 20814
Phone: 301–913–9517; Fax: 301–913–9520

This is a nonprofit, educational organization of endurance athletes and sports medicine professionals. Members receive a monthly newsletter, *Running & FitNews*. The organization distributes brochures and other information to the public about training, nutrition and injury treatment and prevention.

Road Runners Club of America
1150 South Washington Street, Suite 250
Arlington, VA 22314
Phone: 703–836–0558; Fax: 703–836–4430; E-mail: office@rrca.org

This is a nonproftit association of running club members. The national office provides services and information about running to local clubs and the general public. In addition to its quarterly newsletter, *FootNotes*, it also produces brochures on children's running and other topics.

USA Track & Field
P.O. Box 120
Indianapolis, IN 46206
Phone: 317–261–0500; Fax: 317–261–0481

This is the national governing body for track and field, road running and racewalking in the U.S. Its various committees and local associations administer running events and regulations. It also maintains race records, including age-group rankings.

THE INTERNET

User Groups

rec.running
rec.running (access via newsgroups on the Internet)

This discussion group focuses on sharing training advice. Members also discuss shoes, races and trends within distance running.

track and field group
owner-t-and-f@darkwing.uoregon.edu

This discussion group focuses on sharing results and analyzing top-level road, track and cross-country races.

dead runners society
http://storm.cadcam.:upu:.ed:/drs/drs.html

This discussion group focuses on sharing tales of recent running adventures of its members. Participants often seek out members at races when they're traveling.

World Wide Web Pages

Runner's World (updated daily by the magazine's staff)
http://www.runnersworld.com

"Yahoo" (a great starting point—a listing of other Web sites)
http://www.yahoo.com/Recreation/Sports/Running

"The Running Page" (very slick Web page with articles and links to other spots)
http://sunsite.unc.edu/drears/running/running.html

Internet Running Related Sources (Use this URL to go straight to "The Running Page's" links to other sites.)
http://sunsite.unc.edu/drears/running/www.html

Internet Resources for Runners (another good general running pit stop)
http://www.nauticom.net/users/kenecon

"Running Stats Home Page" (current reports on road races around the country)
http://rainbow.rmii.com/~benjid/rs.html

"X-Country Analysis Information" (analysis and news on cross country across the country)
http://www.cs.uml.edu/~phoffman/xc.html

"The Endurance Training Journal" (an online magazine on endurance-sport training)
http://s2.com:80/etj

"Dr. Pribut's Sports Page" (information and advice on sports injuries)
http://www.clark.net/pub/pribut/spsport.html

"RunChat!"(interactive chat system)
http://www.4-lane.com/sportschat

"Athletics Home Page" (world records and statistics for many different countries)
http://www.hkkk.fi/~niininen/athl.html

"College XC-Track Info/Reviews" (Find out how your school is doing this year.)
http://www.cs.uml.edu:80/~phoffman/college.html

"The Athletics Statistics Page" (interesting and offbeat track-and-field statistics)
http://www.users.interport.net/~bricklan/athletic/athletic.html

A BRIEF RUNNING BIBLIOGRAPHY

TRAINING

How to Train for and Run your Best Marathon
by Gordon Bakoulis
Fireside Press, 1230 Avenue of the Americas, New York, NY 10036

An overview of all aspects of training for the marathon. The author placed eighth in the 1992 Women's Olympic Marathon Trials and is the health editor for *Women's Day.*

***Crosstraining* by Gordon Bakoulis**
Fireside Press, 1230 Avenue of the Americas, New York, NY 10036

Examines how and why endurance athletes can combine activities to better their performance in aerobic sports and remain injury free.

***Training Distance Runners* by David Martin, Ph.D. and Peter Coe**
Leisure Press, P. O. Box 5076, Champaign, IL 61825

Science and schedules for top-level racing, from 800 meters through the marathon.

***Lore of Running* by Tim Noakes, MD**
Leisure Press, P. O. Box 5076, Champaign, IL 61825

A compendium of history, training advice, exercise science and injury treatment and avoidance.

***Masters Running and Racing* by Bill Rodgers and Priscilla Welch with Joe Henderson**
Rodale Press, 33 East Minor Street, Emmaus, PA 18098

Advice on running well past the age of 40 by two masters record holders.

***Joan Samuelson's Running for Women* by Joan Benoit Samuelson and Gloria Averbuch**
Rodale Press, 33 East Minor Street, Emmaus, PA 18098

Advice on all facets of running for women by an Olympic Marathon gold medalist.

SPORTS MEDICINE AND NUTRITION

***The Sports Medicine Bible* by Lyle J. Micheli, M.D., with Mark Jenkins**
HarperCollins Publishers, 10 East 53rd Street, New York, NY 10022

How to prevent, detect, and treat your sports injuries by the former president of the American College of Sports

Medicine. Focuses on overuse injuries—the bane of the modern runner.

Power Foods **by Liz Applegate, Ph.D.**
Rodale Press, 33 East Minor Street, Emmaus, PA 18098

Practical information for busy endurance athletes on how to eat for top health and performance.

The Athlete's Kitchen **by Nancy Clark, M.S., R.D.**
Leisure Press, P.O. Box 5076, Champaign, IL 61825

Real-world advice on eating to win from a leading sport nutritionist. Contains many recipes.

Conquering Athletic Injuries **edited by Paul Taylor and Diane Taylor**
Leisure Press, P.O. Box 5076, Champaign, IL 61825

An illustrated guide to diagnosing, treating, and avoiding a vast array of sports injuries.

HISTORY AND BIOGRAPHY

Boston Marathon: The History of the World's Premier Running Event **by Tom Derderian**
Leisure Press, P.O. Box 5076, Champaign, IL 61825

A year-by-year account of the world's most famous road race.

Best Efforts **by Kenny Moore**
Tafnews Press, 2570 El Camino Real, Suite 606, Mountain View, CA 94040

A collection of loving, insightful profiles of leading runners of the 1970s and '80s.

***Pre!* by Tom Jordan**
Tafnews Press, 2570 El Camino Real, Suite 606, Mountain View, CA 94040

The best biography of Steve Prefontaine, the American record holder who died in a car crash at age 24.

***Runners and Other Dreamers* by John L. Parker Jr.**
Cedarwinds Publishing, P.O. Box 351, Medway, OH 45341

A collection of unconventional profiles of leading runners of the 1970s.

***Running with the Legends* by Michael Sandrock**
Leisure Press, P.O. Box 5076, Champaign, IL 61825

In-depth profiles of 21 leading runners of the past 40 years, plus training advice from the elites.

INSPIRATION

***Once A Runner* by John L. Parker Jr.**
Cedarwinds Publishing, P.O. Box 351, Medway, OH 45341

Often called the greatest running novel, this is an accurate and moving story of top runners sacrificing everything to succeed.

***The Runner's Literary Companion* edited by Garth Battista**
Breakaway Books, P.O. Box 1109, Ansonia Station, New York, NY 10023

A hodgepodge of prose and poetry about running. Contains some unexpected authors, such as Walt Whitman and Joyce Carol Oates.

***Thirty Phone Booths to Boston* by Don Kardong**
Penguin USA, 375 Hudson Street, New York, NY 10014

A collection of humorous columns by an Olympic marathoner as he moves through the world as a bemused spectator.

***Hills, Hawgs and Ho Chi Minh* by Don Kardong**
Keokee Publishing, P.O. Box 722, Sandpoint, ID 83864

A more-recent collection of essays by Kardong that play up his love for adventure runs.

***Running and Being* by George Sheehan, M.D.**
Simon & Schuster, Rockefeller Center, 1230 Avenue of the Americas, New York, NY 10020

The standard on the meaning of being a runner in the context of the rest of one's life.

PERFORMANCE TABLES

MEN'S RACE TABLE

This table was created by Donn Kirk, a retired NASA scientist currently in the physics department at the University of Oregon. Kirk created the table using data supplied by Ben Grundstein of Forest Park, NY. It is based on comprehensive results from races conducted by the New York Road Runners Club. Read across the chart for equal performances at standard race distances.

Table of Equal Performances (Men's)

1500m	*1M*	*2M*	*5K*	*4M*	*5M*	*10K*	*12K*	*10M*	*13.1M*	*25K*	*30K*	*26.2M*
3:42.0	4:00.0	8:43.5	14:05.4	18:28	23:25	29:28	35:36	48:31	1:04:47	1:17:58	1:35:14	2:19:26
3:46.1	4:04.4	8:53.0	14:20.8	18:49	23:51	30:00	36:15	49:24	1:06:00	1:19:26	1:37:06	2:22:30
3:53.6	4:12.5	9:10.8	14:49.5	19:26	24:38	31:00	37:28	51:04	1:08:14	1:22:11	1:40:35	2:28:17
4:01.1	4:20.7	9:28.6	15:18.2	20:04	25:26	32:00	38:40	52:43	1:10:29	1:24:56	1:44:05	2:34:07
4:08.7	4:28.8	9:46.3	15:46.9	20:41	26:14	33:00	39:53	54:22	1:12:44	1:27:42	1:47:36	2:40:01
4:16.2	4:37.0	10:04.1	16:15.6	21:19	27:02	34:00	41:05	56:01	1:14:59	1:30:28	1:51:07	2:45:59
4:23.7	4:53.3	10:39.6	17:13.0	22:34	28:37	36:00	43:30	59:19	1:19:29	1:36:02	1:58:13	2:58:07
4:38.8	5:01.4	10:57.4	17:41.7	23:12	29:25	37:00	44:43	1:00:59	1:21:44	1:38:49	2:01:48	3:04:17
4:46.3	5:09.6	11:15.2	18:10.4	23:50	30:12	38:00	45:55	1:02:38	1:24:00	1:41:37	2:05:23	3:10:31
4:53.9	5:17.7	11:32.9	18:39.1	24:27	31:00	39:00	47:08	1:04:17	1:26:16	1:44:25	2:09:00	3:16:48
5:01.4	5:25.8	11:50.7	19:07.8	25:05	31:48	40:00	48:20	1:05:56	1:28:32	1:47:13	2:12:37	3:23:10
5:08.9	5:34.0	12:08.5	19:36.5	25:42	32:35	41:00	49:33	1:07:36	1:30:48	1:50:02	2:16:15	3:29:36
5:16.5	5:42.1	12:26.2	20:05.2	26:20	33:23	42:00	50:45	1:09:15	1:33:04	1:52:51	2:19:54	3:36:05
5:24.0	5:50.3	12:44.0	20:33.8	26:58	34:11	43:00	51:58	1:10:54	1:35:21	1:55:41	2:23:34	3:42:39

1500m	1M	2M	5K	4M	5M	10K	12K	10M	13.1M	25K	30K	26.2M
5:31.5	5:58.4	13:01.8	21:02.5	27:35	34:58	44:00	53:10	1:12:34	1:37:37	1:58:31	2:27:15	3:49:16
5:39.1	6:06.6	13:19.5	21:31.2	28:13	35:46	45:00	54:22	1:14:13	1:39:54	2:01:22	2:30:58	3:55:58
5:46.6	6:14.7	13:37.3	21:59.9	28:51	36:34	46:00	55:35	1:15:52	1:42:11	2:04:12	2:34:40	4:02:43
5:54.1	6:22.9	13:55.1	22:28.6	29:28	37:21	47:00	56:47	1:17:32	1:44:28	2:07:04	2:38:24	4:09:33
6:01.7	6:31.0	14:12.8	22:57.3	30:06	38:09	48:00	58:00	1:19:11	1:46:45	2:09:55	2:42:09	4:16:26
6:09.2	6:39.2	14:30.6	23:26.0	30:43	38:57	49:00	59:12	1:20:51	1:49:03	2:12:47	2:45:55	4:23:23
6:16.8	6:47.3	14:48.4	23:54.7	31:21	39:45	50:00	1:00:25	1:22:30	1:51:20	2:15:40	2:49:42	4:30:24
6:24.3	6:55.5	15:06.1	24:23.4	31:59	40:32	51:00	1:01:37	1:24:10	1:53:38	2:18:32	2:53:29	4:37:30
6:31.8	7:03.6	15:23.9	24:52.1	32:36	41:20	52:00	1:02:50	1:25:49	1:55:56	2:21:26	2:57:18	4:44:39
6:39.4	7:11.7	15:41.7	25:20.8	33:14	42:08	53:00	1:04:02	1:27:29	1:58:14	2:24:19	3:01:07	4:51:52
6:46.9	7:19.9	15:59.4	25:49.5	33:52	42:55	54:00	1:05:15	1:29:08	2:00:32	2:27:13	3:04:58	4:59:09
6:54.4	7:28.0	16:17.2	26:18.2	34:29	43:43	55:00	1:06:27	1:30:48	2:02:51	2:30:08	3:08:49	5:06:30
7:02.0	7:36.2	16:35.0	26:46.9	35:07	44:31	56:00	1:07:40	1:32:27	2:05:09	2:33:02	3:12:42	5:13:55
7:09.5	7:44.3	16:52.7	27:15.6	35:44	45:18	57:00	1:08:52	1:34:07	2:07:28	2:35:57	3:16:35	5:21:23
7:17.0	7:52.5	17:10.5	27:44.3	36:22	46:06	58:00	1:10:04	1:35:47	2:09:47	2:38:53	3:20:29	5:28:56
7:24.6	8:00.6	17:28.3	28:13.0	37:00	46:54	59:00	1:11:17	1:37:26	2:12:06	2:41:49	3:24:25	5:36:33
7:32.1	8:08.8	17:46.1	28:41.6	37:37	47:41	1:00:00	1:12:29	1:39:06	2:14:25	2:44:45	3:28:21	5:44:14
7:39.6	8:16.9	18:03.8	29:10.3	38:15	48:29	1:01:00	1:13:42	1:40:46	2:16:44	2:47:42	3:32:18	5:51:58
7:47.2	8:25.1	18:21.6	29:39.0	38:53	49:17	1:02:00	1:14:54	1:42:25	2:19:04	2:50:39	3:36:16	5:59:47
7:54.7	8:33.2	18:39.4	30:07.7	39:30	50:05	1:03:00	1:16:07	1:44:05	2:21:24	2:53:37	3:40:15	6:07:39
8:02.2	8:41.4	18:57.1	30:36.4	40:08	50:52	1:04:00	1:17:19	1:45:45	2:23:43	2:56:34	3:44:15	6:15:36

WOMEN'S RACE TABLE

This table was created by Donn Kirk, a retired NASA scientist currently in the physics department at the University of Oregon. Kirk created the table using data supplied by Ben Grundstein of Forest Park, NY. It is based on comprehensive results from races conducted by the New York Road Runners Club. Read across the chart for equal performances at standard race distances.

Table of Equal Performances (Women's)

1500m	*1M*	*2M*	*5K*	*4M*	*5M*	*10K*	*12K*	*10M*	*13.1M*	*25K*	*30K*	*26.2M*
4:22.8	4:44.1	10:11.1	16:18.6	21:19	27:00	34:00	41:16	56:27	1:15:32	1:30:46	1:50:39	2:40:31
4:30.5	4:52.5	10:29.2	16:47.4	21:57	27:48	35:00	42:29	58:07	1:17:47	1:33:30	1:54:05	2:45:54
4:38.3	5:00.9	10:47.2	17:16.2	22:35	28:36	36:00	43:41	59:47	1:20:02	1:36:15	1:57:30	2:51:18
4:46.0	5:09.2	11:05.3	17:44.9	23:12	29:23	37:00	44:54	1:01:26	1:22:17	1:38:59	2:00:56	2:56:45
4:53.7	5:17.6	11:22.3	18:13.7	23:50	30:11	38:00	46:08	1:03:07	1:24:32	1:41:43	2:04:20	3:02:15
5:01.5	5:25.9	11:41.4	18:42.5	24:28	30:59	39:00	47:19	1:04:46	1:26:47	1:44:29	2:07:49	3:07:46
5:09.2	5:34.3	11:59.5	19:11.3	25:06	31:46	40:00	48:32	1:06:25	1:29:02	1:47:14	2:11:17	3:13:20
5:16.9	5:42.7	12:17.6	19:40.1	25:43	32:34	41:00	49:45	1:08:06	1:31:18	1:50:00	2:14:46	3:18:55
5:24.6	5:51.0	12:35.6	20:08.8	26:21	33:22	42:00	50:57	1:09:45	1:33:33	1:52:46	2:18:14	3:24:34
5:32.4	5:59.4	12:53.7	20:37.6	26:59	34:09	43:00	52:10	1:11:25	1:35:49	1:55:32	2:21:44	3:30:14
5:40.1	6:07.7	13:11.8	21:06.4	27:37	34:57	44:00	53:23	1:13:05	1:38:04	1:58:18	2:25:13	3:35:57
5:47.8	6:16.1	13:29.9	21:35.2	28:14	35:45	45:00	54:35	1:14:45	1:40:20	2:01:05	2:28:43	3:41:41
5:55.6	6:24.4	13:47.9	22:04.0	28:52	36:32	46:00	55:48	1:16:25	1:42:36	2:03:52	2:32:14	3:47:28
6:03.3	6:32.8	14:06.0	22:32.8	29:30	37:20	47:00	57:01	1:18:04	1:44:52	2:06:39	2:35:46	3:53:18
6:11.0	6:41.2	14:24.2	23:01.5	30:08	38:08	48:00	58:13	1:19:44	1:47:07	2:09:25	2:39:17	3:59:09

1500m	1M	2M	5K	4M	5M	10K	12K	10M	13.1M	25K	30K	26.2M
6:18.8	6:49.5	14:42.3	23:30.3	30:45	38:55	49:00	59:26	1:21:24	1:49:23	2:12:12	2:42:49	4:05:03
6:26.5	6:57.9	15:00.4	23:59.1	31:23	39:43	50:00	1:00:38	1:23:04	1:51:40	2:15:01	2:46:23	4:10:59
6:34.2	7:06.2	15:18.5	24:27.9	32:01	40:31	51:00	1:01:51	1:24:44	1:53:56	2:17:48	2:49:57	4:16:57
6:41.9	7:14.6	15:36.6	24:56.7	32:39	41:19	52:00	1:03:04	1:26:23	1:56:12	2:20:36	2:53:31	4:22:58
6:49.7	7:22.9	15:54.7	25:25.4	33:17	42:06	53:00	1:04:16	1:28:03	1:58:28	2:23:24	2:57:05	4:29:01
6:57.4	7:31.3	16:12.8	25:54.2	33:54	42:54	54:00	1:05:29	1:29:43	2:00:45	2:26:13	3:00:41	4:35:06
7:05.1	7:39.7	16:31.0	26:23.0	34:32	43:42	55:00	1:06:41	1:31:23	2:03:01	2:29:01	3:04:16	4:41:13
7:12.9	7:48.0	16:49.1	26:51.8	35:10	44:29	56:00	1:07:54	1:33:03	2:05:18	2:31:51	3:07:52	4:47:22
7:20.6	7:56.4	17:07.3	27:20.6	35:48	45:17	57:00	1:09:06	1:34:43	2:07:35	2:34:40	3:11:30	4:53:34
7:28.3	8:04.7	17:25.4	27:49.4	36:26	46:05	58:00	1:10:19	1:36:22	2:09:51	2:37:28	3:15:06	4:59:48
7:36.1	8:13.1	17:43.6	28:18.1	37:03	46:52	59:00	1:11:31	1:38:02	2:12:08	2:40:18	3:18:44	5:06:04
7:43.8	8:21.4	18:01.7	28:46.9	37:41	47:40	1:00:00	1:12:44	1:39:42	2:14:25	2:43:08	3:22:23	5:12:23
7:51.5	8:29.8	18:19.9	29:15.7	38:19	48:28	1:01:00	1:13:56	1:41:22	2:16:42	2:45:58	3:26:02	5:18:43
7:59.2	8:38.2	18:38.1	29:44.5	38:57	49:15	1:02:00	1:15:09	1:43:02	2:18:59	2:48:48	3:29:41	5:25:06
8:07.0	8:46.5	18:56.2	30:13.3	39:35	50:03	1:03:00	1:16:21	1:44:41	2:21:16	2:51:39	3:33:21	5:31:31
8:14.7	8:54.9	19:14.4	30:42.0	40:12	50:51	1:04:00	1:17:34	1:46:22	2:23:34	2:54:30	3:37:03	5:37:59
8:22.4	9:03.2	19:32.5	31:10.8	40:50	51:38	1:05:00	1:18:46	1:48:01	2:25:51	2:57:21	3:40:43	5:44:28
8:30.2	9:11.6	19:50.7	31:39.6	41:28	52:26	1:06:00	1:19:59	1:49:41	2:28:09	3:00:13	3:44:26	5:51:00
8:37.9	9:19.9	20:08.9	32:08.4	42:06	53:14	1:07:00	1:21:11	1:51:21	2:30:26	3:03:03	3:48:07	5:57:34
8:45.6	9:28.3	20:27.1	32:37.2	42:44	54:02	1:08:00	1:22:24	1:53:01	2:32:44	3:05:56	3:51:50	6:04:10
8:53.3	9:36.7	20:45.4	33:06.0	43:22	54:49	1:09:00	1:23:36	1:54:41	2:35:01	3:08:47	3:55:33	6:10:49
9:01.1	9:45.0	21:03.5	33:34.7	44:00	55:37	1:10:00	1:24:49	1:56:21	2:37:19	3:11:39	3:59:17	6:17:30
9:08.8	9:53.4	21:21.7	34:03.5	44:38	56:25	1:11:00	1:26:01	1:58:01	2:39:37	3:14:31	4:03:02	6:24:13

This chart was produced by Ben Grundstein of Forest Park, NY. It lists the average performance at New York Road Runners Club events during 1995 by distance and age group.

Average Performances at Standard Race Distances by Age Group

Average Times for 1995 New York Road Runners Club Races in 1995—Men

	5K	5M	10K	10M	13.1M	26.2M
Age 0–14	25:34	44:07	49:43	1:17:11	2:04:24	—
Age 15–19	21:23	36:04	44:48	1:11:08	1:36:03	4:21:57
Age 20–29	23:29	37:23	45:45	1:13:40	1:43:27	4:14:44
Age 30–39	23:59	38:05	47:26	1:16:32	1:45:14	4:14:32
Age 40–44	24:40	39:30	49:12	1:19:13	1:49:00	4:22:21
Age 45–49	25:24	40:16	49:06	1:21:29	1:51:20	4:30:57
Age 50–54	25:36	42:43	51:40	1:26:46	1:53:02	4:39:40
Age 55–59	26:43	43:39	52:56	1:25:28	2:01:25	4:53:04
Age 60–64	28:29	43:39	53:46	1:25:43	2:06:20	5:04:59
Age 65–69	27:58	43:56	53:43	1:33:43	2:06:22	5:34:49
Age 70–74	27:49	46:21	1:00:28	1:43:36	2:07:22	5:56:27
Age 75+	35:40	54:47	1:11:58	2:07:10	2:40:32	6:21:32

Average Times for 1995 New York Road Runners Club Races in 1995—Women

	5K	5M	10K	10M	13.1M	26.2 M
Age 0–14	30:48	52:01	53:24	—	1:48:40	—
Age 15–19	29:20	42:23	53:47	1:24:32	2:01:16	5:15:12
Age 20–29	28:20	44:39	55:17	1:27:02	2:00:07	4:39:45
Age 30–39	29:02	45:02	55:49	1:27:54	2:00:44	4:44:39
Age 40–44	29:54	46:59	56:30	1:29:15	2:03:20	4:59:58
Age 45–49	32:22	50:06	59:48	1:35:39	2:08:25	5:17:39
Age 50–54	31:34	48:25	58:26	1:33:11	2:11:31	5:26:31
Age 55–59	34:38	49:24	1:01:46	1:34:28	2:16:47	5:56:14
Age 60–64	31:46	54:45	1:05:23	1:38:48	2:15:28	5:52:30
Age 65–69	36:59	51:49	1:02:40	1:32:19	2:18:52	6:31:52
Age 70+	39:45	1:03:09	1:15:12	1:49:20	2:51:07	6:22:14

INDEX